-FIRE

Km.

ENDER

OR

AK TANKS, OIL DUMPS IN CHHAMB

OSTS

dead...
depots
kilo-
tor.

WITHIN F...

TANGAIL, LAKHIMPUR & SITAKUND LIBERATED

Advance Toward Chittagong Being Maintained

NEW DELHI, Dec. 13 (PTI, UND.– The Indian Army columns racing towards Dacca from three directions were this evening within artillery range of the West Pakistan occupation forces of a division plus trapped in the Bangla Desh capital, an official spokesman said tonight.

AF194620

Pak Sabre Bombed Orphanage

23 POSTS UNDER OUR CONTROL IN KARGIL SECTOR

UDHAMPUR, Dec. 13 (PTI & UND. – The overall situation all along the 600 miles of the so-called cease-fire

UK To Keep Up Arms Supplies Despite War

Evacuation
The Purpo...
Says Delhi

CHIEF MINISTER
G. M. SADIQ
PASSES AWAY

From Our Staff Representative

CHANDIGARH, Dec. 12 – The Jammu an Kashmir Chief Minister, Mr. Ghulam Mohamm Sadiq, passed away at the P.G.I. here today.

The wrapped body of Kashmir Chief Minister G. M. Sadiq being taken out of the PGI, Chandigarh, on Sunday by Director P. N. Chhutani and others.

Heavy Fighting Raging Near
Dacca And Khulna

CALCUTTA, Decem ber 12 (UNI) — Fighting w... and the key district town of Khulna, as column... gia Desh forces continued to close in on the capital of Chittagong.

INDIAN TROOPS LIBERAT...

INDIAN TROOPS LIBERAT...

ENEMY DEFENCE
LINES SMASHED

BULK OF PAK FORCES
GIVE UP FIGHT, FLEEING

CALCUTTA, Dec. 8 (PTI) — Combined forces of the Indian Army and Mukti Bahini scored yet another sig- nal victory in smashing the Pakistani defence lines and liberating Comilla town today.

The joint columns in the early hours today liberated the Comilla air- field and took hold of the Lalmai heights in a swift move, cutting off all avenues of escape to Mynamati Cantonment, an Eastern Command spo- kesman told newsmen here tonight.

CEASE-FIRE LINE

KASHMIR

PAKISTAN

PAK HELD KASHMIR

NAYA CHHOR AIRFIELD IN

IAF gains total air supremacy in Bangla Desh

ECOGNISES

HISTORI
GREETE
M.P.s Congrat...
Fulfillin
OTHER NATIONS
SUIT...

IAF gains total air supremacy in Bangla Desh

E FIGHTI...
E ENEMY
S RE...
INDIAN ARMY
Gai
l Se
(PTI) – A
ENEMY

'E. PAK' CABINET
MALIK'S HOUSE
DESTROYED

Over 2,000 sq. k...
Captured In...

Indian Troops Blast Their
Way Into Dacca's Outskirts

DACCA, December 14 (Reuter) — The Government of 'East Pakistan' resigned en masse this afternoon, dissociating itself from further action of central administration of President Yahya Khan in Islamabad as Indian troops blasted their way into the outskirts of Dacca.

Mr. A. M. Malik, the 'Governor', wrote from his Cabinet resign- ation letter to President Yahya with a shaking ball point pen on a sheet of office paper as Indian MIG 21s destroyed his official residence.

Troops Close
On Dac...

Surrounded by his Minis...
from Mr. Malik shows a...
draft to United Nations...
John Kelly and J...
Young of the London...
Observer, who had...
stopped with him in...
bunker by an air raid...

NEW DELHI, Dec. 7 (UNI)
neous moves in
MORE

SE-FIRE

2 Km.

RRENDER

PAK TANKS, OIL DUMPS IN CHHAMB

POSTS

CTOR

flicted "dead-
ration depots
eight kilo-
amb sector.

seeks

inary

Heavy Fighting Raging Near
Dacca And Khulna

RECOGNISES

HISTOR
GREETE
M.P.s Congrat
Fulfillin
OTHER NATIONS
SUIT

TANGAIL, LAKHIMPUR & SITAKUND LIBERATED

Advance Toward Chittagong Being Maintained

NEW DELHI, Dec. 13 (PTI, UNI).— The Indian Army columns racing towards Dacca from three directions were this evening within artillery range of the West Pakistan occupation forces of a division plus trapped in the Bangla Desh capital, an official spokesman said tonight.

WITHIN FIRING RANGE OF IND

Evacuati

Pak Sabre
Bombed
Orphanage

23 POSTS UNDER
OUR CONTROL IN
KARGIL SECTOR

UK To Kee
Up Arms
Supplies
Despite War

UDHAMPUR, Dec. 13 (PTI & UNI).— The overall situation all along the 600 miles of the

CHIEF MINISTER
G. M. SADIQ
PASSES AWAY

From Our Staff Representative

CHANDIGARH, Dec. 12 — The Jammu an
Kashmir Chief Minister, Mr. Ghulam Mohamme
Sadiq, passed away at the P.G.I. here today

The wrapped body of Kashmir Chief Minister G. M. Sadiq is being taken out of the PGI, Chandigarh, on Sunday by Director P. N. Chhuttani and others.

INDIAN TROOPS LIBERA

ENEMY DEFENCE
LINES SMASHED

BULK OF PAK FORCES
GIVE UP FIGHT, FLEEING

CALCUTTA, Dec. 8 (PTI) — Combined forces of the Indian Army and Mukti Bahini scored yet another sig-nal victory in smashing the Pakistani defence lines and liberating Comilla town today.

The joint columns in the early hours today liberated the Comilla air-field and took hold of the Lalmai heights in a swift move, cutting off all avenues of escape to Mynamati Cantonment, an Eastern Command spo-kesman told newsmen here tonight.

IAF gains total
air supremacy
in Bangla Desh

'E. PAK' CABINET

MALIK'S HOUSE
DESTROYED

Indian Troops Blast Their
Way Into Dacca's Outskirts

DACCA, December 14 (Reuter).— The Government of 'East Pakistan' resigned en masse this afternoon, dissociating itself from further actions of central administration of President Yahya Khan as Indian troops blasted their way into the outskirts of Dacca.

Mr. A. M. Malik, the 'Governor', wrote the draft of his Cabinet resign-ation letter to President Yahya with a shaking ball point pen on a sheet of office paper as Indian MIG 21s destroyed his official residence

CE FIGHTI

IVE ENEMY
CKS REP
INDIAN ARMY

ian Gai
argil Se
ENEMY

ec. 10 (PTI) — A

Troops Close
On Dacc

Over 2,000
Capture

NAYA CHOR

HEROES OF 1971

The effort of *The Tribune* group of newspapers in publishing a collection of articles in the form of a book to mark fifty years of the 1971 India–Pakistan War is commendable. The written accounts showcase the emphatic victory of our armed forces over Pakistan. The articles are authored by several eminent persons, who either participated in the operations or have carried out research on the leadership and conduct of the war. These writings will serve as a tribute to the gallantry of all those who were part of the historic war effort.

– General Bipin Rawat, PVSM, UYSM, AVSM, YSM, SM, VSM, ADC; Chief of the Defence Staff

It is heartening to learn that *The Tribune* group of newspapers is publishing a collection of articles in the form of a book to mark 50 years of the 1971 India–Pakistan war. These articles, written by the country's defence writers, including retired and serving defence services officers, commentators and analysts, will serve as a tribute to the gallantry of our officers and men.

– General MM Naravane, PVSM, AVSM, SM, VSM, ADC; Chief of the Army Staff

I am pleased that *The Tribune* and HarperCollins have taken the initiative to publish a series of articles in the form of a book to mark 50 years of the 1971 India–Pakistan War. Written by the country's top defence writers and analysts, these articles will serve as a tribute to the gallantry of all air warriors. For the Indian Air Force, the 'Golden Hour' of the IAF has been aptly captured in the articles on our warriors. My compliments to the team and best wishes for the future.

– Air Chief Marshal VR Chaudhari, PVSM, AVSM, VM, ADC;
Chief of the Air Staff

Adroit planning, joint employment of combat power, and tactical ingenuity of the Indian Armed Forces in the 1971 Indo-Pak war added a golden chapter in India's history, and altered the geography of the South Asian subcontinent. This captivating compilation of articles encapsulates the selfless sacrifice and acts of bravery by our armed forces. The section on Param Vir Chakra and Maha Vir Chakra awardees highlights their gallantry in the face of adversity and would act as an inspiration to younger generations. The naval battles during the war have been evocatively covered, highlighting some of the finest moments in Indian Navy's history. On the occasion of Swarnim Vijay Varsh, this publication aptly commemorates our victory and pays homage to our valiant soldiers, sailors, and air-warriors.

– Admiral Karambir Singh, PVSM, AVSM, ADC;
Chief of the Naval Staff

HEROES OF 1971

THE BRAVEHEARTS OF THE WAR THAT GAVE BIRTH TO BANGLADESH

EDITED BY RAJESH RAMACHANDRAN

HarperCollins *Publishers* India

First published in India by
HarperCollins *Publishers* 2021
4th Floor, Tower A, Building No. 10, Phase II,
DLF Cyber City, Gurugram, Haryana – 122002
www.harpercollins.co.in

2 4 6 8 10 9 7 5 3 1

P-ISBN: 978-93-5489-321-6
E-ISBN: 978-93-5489-327-8

Cover design: Gavin Morris
Front cover: Alamy
Back cover: Shutterstock
Editor photo: Vijay Pandey

Typeset in 11.5/15.7 Warnock Pro at
Manipal Technologies Limited, Manipal

Printed and bound at
Thomson Press (India) Ltd

 HarperCollinsIn

MIX
Paper
FSC   FSC® C010615

This book is produced from independently certified FSC® paper
to ensure responsible forest management.

Dedicated to all our brave men in uniform and the unsung heroes who laid down their lives to safeguard our country

Contents

Foreword

BRITISH India was partitioned in August 1947 and two free nations were born: India and Pakistan. India celebrates its Independence Day on 15 August every year, and for Pakistan, it is a day earlier. While India chose to form itself into a sovereign socialist secular republic, our neighbour declared itself as the Islamic Republic of Pakistan. In the months preceding and during the Partition, millions of innocent people were killed in the gruesome communal violence that engulfed the subcontinent. Over 20 million were rendered homeless.

The interim government of India, our first national government, worked day and night to restore law and order across the vast territory from Bengal to Punjab, establishing hundreds of refugee camps to provide shelter, food, clothing and medical care to the millions who had fled from the areas which were to now form the territory of Pakistan. In the midst of this highly disturbed situation, Pakistan, barely a few weeks old as a nation, mobilized armed tribal groups, trained and led by Pakistan army officers out of uniform, and invaded the princely Indian state of Jammu and Kashmir with the objective of 'seizing' it. After months of debate in the United Nations (UN), Pakistan's naked aggression was brought to a stop in late 1948, and the demarcated ceasefire line became effective from July 1949. Over seventy years have since elapsed, and Pakistan religiously continues to pursue its avowed goal of delivering a 'thousand cuts' to dismember India and 'take Kashmir'.

In the early 1950s, at the persuasion of the US, Pakistan joined two security pacts, Southeast Asia Treaty Organization (SEATO) and Central Treaty Organization (CENTO), which enabled it to receive America's continuing support for strengthening and enlarging its military capabilities. Needless to say, this arrangement provided the US the opportunity to have a presence in Pakistan and exercise growing influence over its defence and foreign policies. Meanwhile, India eschewed involvement in any security-related agreements with other countries and remained firmly committed to its policy of seeking peaceful and friendly relations with all its neighbours.

In 1965, Pakistan launched Operation Gibraltar with the objective of infiltrating trained terrorists in large numbers into J&K and perpetrating a massive insurgency, which they thought would ensure India's ouster from Kashmir. While this adventure failed, Pakistan continued its cross-border skirmishes, which finally led to the 1965 war with India. The hostilities ended with a UN Security Council (UNSC)-enabled ceasefire, followed by the Tashkent Declaration, which was engendered by the diplomatic intervention of the Soviet Union. India agreed to the ceasefire when it was in occupation of over 1,900 sq. km of enemy territory. However, Pakistan claimed victory over India and widely drummed that it had won the backing of the entire international community in countering India's 'aggression'.

While India had, since Independence, remained intensively engaged in tackling the challenges of nation-building and placing its democratic framework on a firm footing, the governance of Pakistan had, since 1958, firmly settled in the hands of its military generals, who were openly opposed to democracy.

Pakistan's eastern wing, East Pakistan, lay 1,600 km away from West Pakistan. In terms of growth and development, it had suffered adversely for many years because of the highly discriminatory policies of the federal government of Pakistan, which had refused to provide the much-needed political and economic support to East Pakistan. As unashamedly pronounced by the commanding Pakistani generals, one of the reasons for their harsh treatment of the people of East Bengal was because they 'were not Urdu but Bengali speaking', and worse still, 'followed socio-cultural practices which were common with those practised by the people living in the neighbouring states of India'. Briefly, they were saying that because the people of East Pakistan spoke Bengali and conformed to socio-cultural traditions followed by Hindus in India, the people of East Pakistan were to be considered as 'infidels' who did not deserve to be treated as Pakistanis and, as such, deserved to be 'given the boot'.

Elections to the Pakistan National Assembly, held in December 1970, had resulted in the Awami League, the main political party in East Pakistan led by Sheikh Mujibur Rahman, sweeping the polls. At that time, Pakistan was ruled by President Yahya Khan. Notwithstanding the clear victory of the Awami League, Yahya Khan ensured that Sheikh Mujibur Rahman was denied the opportunity to form the next government. This objective was secured, inter alia, by repeatedly postponing the date for convening the National Assembly. In early March 1971, the Pakistan government brazenly announced that the National Assembly would not be convened for an 'indefinite' period. This unconstitutional decision triggered violent protests and riots across the length and breadth of East Bengal, whose people had suffered discrimination and endless atrocities for far too long and their patience had been exhausted. This fresh wave of protests by the oppressed people marked the beginning of the 'freedom movement' in East Bengal.

In end March 1971, to bring East Bengal under tighter control and to teach its people a lesson, General Tikka Khan, Chief of Pakistan Army's Eastern Command, launched 'Operation Searchlight'. The ensuing crackdown all over East Bengal led to the Pakistani military indulging in arson, rape, loot and large-scale genocidal massacres, for which Tikka Khan came to be known as the 'Butcher of Bangladesh'. The wave of terror created by the genocidal killings led to people fleeing their homes to save their lives. This triggered a massive exodus to the neighbouring Indian states, and by the end of November

1971, nearly 10 million Bangladeshis had crossed over to India. This enormous influx caused serious political, economic and security problems for the host states in India. The government of India made continuing diplomatic attempts, through various possible channels, to secure an arrangement with Pakistan under which these refugees could return home on their own terms (and not on any proposed by India). All its efforts failed. India was faced with a grave financial crisis, and besides, serious security problems; a rapidly increasing number of incidents of sabotage, subversion and communal tension were being perpetrated by Pakistani Inter-Services Intelligence (ISI) agents, who had succeeded in crossing over by mingling with the large groups of Bangladeshis who had entered India.

The situation in East Pakistan continued to remain highly disturbed. The ranks of the Mukti Bahini, a militant organization which had emerged to liberate East Pakistan, were strengthened by a large number of patriotic elements who deserted the Pakistan army and paramilitary forces to join the Bangladeshi freedom movement. The Mukti Bahini provided invaluable strength to the freedom struggle by imparting military training to a large number of volunteers from among the people. These trained persons were formed into small fighting units, which successfully carried out guerrilla attacks to destroy roads and bridges, communication centres and vital military installations.

Despite the mounting insurgency in East Pakistan, the Pakistan army maintained a largely defensive posture in the east. However, it moved rapidly to build a substantially offensive profile along its western wing, with the objective of launching surprise operations to occupy important Indian territories (in the west) to make up for its likely losses in the east. This was in pursuit of its known policy of 'defence of the east by attacking in the west'.

Pakistan continued to build up the tenor of its widespread propaganda campaign to create a false impression worldwide that India was preparing to attack East Pakistan any time to dismember the Islamic state of Pakistan. Under this semblance, Pakistan sought sympathy, financial aid and military support to defend itself against 'India's aggression'. The US came out in open support of Pakistan and provided it the requisite military assistance. President Yahya Khan arranged for Henry Kissinger, National Security Adviser to President Nixon, to undertake a secret visit to Beijing to secure Chinese support. China, which had its own reasons for supporting Pakistan against India, promptly came forth to firm up the US–China nexus against any Indian intervention in East Pakistan. Iran, Jordan and some other countries also offered support to Pakistan.

The very strong support provided by the US and China gave enormous confidence to Pakistan to 'take on' India. Pakistan also believed that, as had happened in its 1965 war against India, the UN would, this time, too, promptly intervene to bring about a ceasefire. This conviction further emboldened Pakistan to enormously step up its genocidal war in East Pakistan and also increase its skirmishes with India.

Indira Gandhi's continued diplomatic efforts through the summer of 1971 to persuade Pakistan to agree to any arrangement under which the millions of East Pakistan refugees could return to their country did not bear any fruit. In October 1971, by which time Pakistan's belligerence had increased manifold, she set out on a tour of France, Germany, Belgium, UK, Australia and the US to personally inform the world about Pakistan's genocide in East Pakistan and the grave economic and security problems which India had been patiently bearing consequent to the inflow of over 10 million Bangladeshis into India. As she had known and expected, she did not receive positive response from any quarter. However, the USSR, with whom India had enjoyed good relations for many years, and with whom Indira Gandhi had signed a Treaty of Peace, Corporation and Friendship in August 1971, strongly supported India's position in the UN and at every other forum.

The mounting hysteria in West Pakistan to wage war against India reached its crescendo on 3 December 1971 when, backed (virtually instigated) by the Washington–Beijing nexus, the Pakistan Air Force (PAF) launched a pre-emptive air strike to destroy air bases and radar stations in north-western India. The Pak bombers penetrated as far deep as Agra, which is at least 500 km from India's border with Pakistan. Side by side, Pakistan launched heavy artillery attacks across the Line of Control (LoC) in J&K.

In a midnight broadcast to the nation, Indira Gandhi declared that Pakistan's hostile air attack a few hours earlier was 'war against India'. After the Prime Minister's statement, India's armed forces immediately moved into action and launched attacks by land, sea and air on targets in Pakistan.

I shall not comment on the course of the conflict or describe the battles won or lost in the 1971 war. The events of the two-front war, which lasted all of thirteen days, are well recorded in several books. The three armed forces of India operated with outstanding cohesion to defeat its US–China-backed adversary on all fronts, taking 93,000 prisoners and securing an unconditional Instrument of Surrender. The people of East

Pakistan and the Mukti Bahini had played an important role in supporting the Indian armed forces to defeat Pakistan.

———

This year we are celebrating the golden jubilee of the 1971 war in which India's military won a glorious victory and liberated the people of East Pakistan from their endless sufferings at the hands of the ruling Pakistani generals. The dismemberment of Pakistan and the birth of Bangladesh changed the geopolitical configuration of the Indian subcontinent and of south Asia.

A very important facet of this war, which has apparently been long since forgotten, is that India, which had very many problems of its own, provided succour to over 10 million Bangladeshis who had fled to India when the Pakistan military unleashed its frenzy of rape, looting and genocidal killings in East Pakistan. And when all of India's diplomatic efforts for the return of these millions of refugees had failed, and with Pakistan launching an air attack on India on 3 December, there was no looking back. India deployed all its military resources to competently defeat Pakistan and liberate the people of East Pakistan to live as free citizens in their own new country, called Bangladesh.

India's famed victory was gained with 4,000 of its soldiers making the supreme sacrifice and 10,000 being injured. The golden jubilee of the 1971 war is a most befitting occasion for the people of India—now more than 1.35 billion—to pay respectful homage to our martyrs and to remember the heroic deeds of the men and officers of our armed forces in that war. Since Independence, the forces have been making endless sacrifices to protect and preserve India's territorial integrity.

In the 1971 war, the scintillating success of our armed forces was due to the very strong leadership of the Army Chief, General SF Manekshaw, and the outstanding operational cohesion that he was able to achieve in concert with the Navy and Air Force Chiefs, Adm. SM Nanda and Air Chief Marshal PC Lal, who were equally tall leaders.

The perfect planning and cohesive execution of operations in this war are a shining example of what in today's terminology is called 'joint war fighting'. The enormous 'jointness' in the functioning of the armed forces was sustained by the truly remarkable politico-military understanding, which obtained during the entire preparatory phase, during the war itself, and even thereafter. Prime Minister Indira Gandhi, backed by her cabinet, provided unstinted support and encouragement to General Manekshaw and the other two Chiefs of Staff. In this task, she was most ably supported by her Defence Minister, Jagjivan Ram, and the Principal Defence Secretary, KB Lall, both of whom performed outstanding behind-the-scenes roles to secure coordination among the three defence services. Besides, they also ensured that the paramilitary forces, particularly the BSF (led by the eminent police officer KF Rustamji), the civil and police administrations in the adjoining states (West Bengal, Assam, Meghalaya and Tripura), and the heads of all other departments and organizations concerned of the central and state governments were fully prepared to discharge their roles without any let or hindrance. And the intelligence inputs were outstandingly harmonized and delivered in good time by RN Kao (an astute former Intelligence Bureau functionary), who had taken over as the founder-head of the Research and Analysis Wing (R&AW) in 1968.

Pakistan's defeat, the birth of Bangladesh, the return of millions of East Pakistani refugees to their new homeland (a very large number stayed behind in India, too), and the significant transformation in the geopolitics of south Asia were truly historical incidents of momentous significance. About all this, regrettably, the present generation knows very little.

It is my strong belief that veritable histories of India's wars must be written up and published without any delay, to be read by one and all.

Regrettably, there have been delays of decades before authorized versions of such events have been released by the government for publication. This procrastination has been at the cost of several generations of our military officers who, while undergoing training in various military academies, were denied the opportunity of studying the histories of past wars to understand the kind of preparatory planning and operational exercises that are required to be carried out jointly by the three defence services if the enemy is to be defeated and India is to win wars.

Another great loss arising from the indefinite delay in the timely publication of military histories has been that the people at large, especially our youth, have remained ignorant of the enormous sacrifices made by the gallant officers and men of our armed forces who have been defending and protecting our frontiers on land, sea and air. It also needs to be remembered that a vital component of national strength is national fervour, which can be gainfully engendered and sustained if our people, particularly the youth, are aware of the serious and recurring security threats that have been faced by our country since Independence. They must know and understand how these challenges were countered, and the reasons for our successes and failures. I would iterate that military histories need to be finalized without delay and placed in the public domain instead of being locked up as 'secret' documents, as our security management apparatus has done in the past decades.

———

With the objective of making its own small contribution towards facilitating the histories of wars being made known to the people at large, *The Tribune* (published from Chandigarh) decided to celebrate the golden jubilee of the 1971 war by publishing stories relating to this conflict, particularly those which recount the heroic deeds of our soldiers—many of whom never returned home—which enabled our military forces to win this war.

The Tribune, over 140 years old today, is the leading English daily newspaper read across the whole of northern India. This region is the catchment, the granary, from where thousands of our youth get enlisted in the defence and paramilitary forces every year. This area is also home to the families of several lakh soldiers, airmen and sailors, both serving and retired. I mention these facts to explain why *The Tribune* is so close to the entire uniformed community and their families.

The Tribune has provided authentic reportage on military matters for well over a century. It closely covered the course of the 1971 war, both on the eastern and western fronts, keeping lakhs of its readers well informed with its detailed daily accounts of the battles that were being fought. And for nearly a year now, the newspaper has been publishing, every Sunday, specially written stories on the significant events of the 1971 war to make its readers aware of the difficulties faced and the sacrifices made by our brave soldiers, the historical role played by India and its armed forces in the dismemberment of Pakistan and the creation of Bangladesh, and changing the geopolitics of the subcontinent.

I believe that it would greatly benefit the nation if copies of this very well-compiled book on the 1971 war were to be made available in libraries all over the country. It would be of even greater value if regional translations of this volume were to be made and distributed free, or at a nominal price, to schools and colleges in the country. This would enable our people, our public servants and our polity to gain a better understanding of the difficult role played by our armed forces in preserving the territorial integrity of our country.

To conclude, I would like to record my appreciation of the efforts made by Rajesh Ramachandran, Editor of *The Tribune*, to make the publication of this volume possible.

NN Vohra
President
The Tribune Trust
Chandigarh
2 November 2021

List of Abbreviations

ASW: Anti-Submarine Warfare
ATGM: Anti-Tank Guided Missiles
AVSM: Ati Vishisht Seva Medal
BOPs: Border Outposts
Brig.: Brigadier
BSF: Border Security Force
CAS: Close Air Support
CCA: Carrier-Controlled Approaches
CFL: Ceasefire Line
CO: Commanding Officer
COAS: Chief of the Army Staff
Col: Colonel

CRPF: Central Reserve Police Force

DBO: Daulat Beg Oldi

DGMO: Director General of Military Operations

FAC: Forward Air Controller

FR: Fighter Reconnaissance

Gen.: General

GOC: General Officer Commanding

GR: Gorkha Rifles

HU: Helicopter Unit

IMA: Indian Military Academy

JBCU: Jet Bomber Conversion Unit

Lt: Lieutenant

LMG: Light Machine Gun

LoC: Line of Control

LS: Leading Seaman

Maj.: Major

MMGs: Medium Machine Guns

MOPs: Mobile Observation Posts

MVC: Maha Vir Chakra

NDA: National Defence Academy

NDC: National Defence College

OBE: Order of British Empire

Op.: Operation

OTU: Operational Training Unit

PAF: Pakistan Air Force

PoK: Pakistan-occupied Kashmir

PVSM: Param Vishisht Seva Medal

PVC: Param Vir Chakra

R/T: Radio Transmission

RCL: Recoil-Less

RL: Rocket Launcher

RO: Reviewing Officer

SSG: Special Service Group

TAC: Tactical Air Centre

TACDE: Tactics and Air Combat Development Establishment

TNT: Trinitrotoluene

UNSC: United Nations Security Council

USAF: United States Air Force

USSR: Union of Soviet Socialist Republics

Wg Cdr: Wing Commander

50 YEARS OF THE 1971 WAR

The March to Free Dhaka

Lt Gen. SS Mehta (Retd)

Former Western Army Commander Lt Gen. SS Mehta (Retd), who as a greenhorn commanded a tank squadron that rolled into Dhaka, remembers the epic battles that were fought beyond the brief

IT is now only a four-hour journey by road, but fifty years ago, the Akhaura-to-Dhaka march that redrew the map of south Asia and rewrote its military history took us thirteen tumultuous days. After a brilliant seventy-two-hour operation at Akhaura, the enemy's formidable stronghold—defended by a battalion of Pakistan's elite 12 Frontier Force and elements of 12 Azad Kashmir, supported by tanks, artillery and air service—wilted, and whatever was left of them was in retreat.

The credit for this remarkable victory goes to the 311 Mountain Brigade Group, commanded by Brig. RN Mishra. The operation was a brilliant success, with 4 Guards, commanded by the dashing and inspirational Lt Col Himmeth Singh, infiltrating the enemy lines, and the lead company, commanded by Maj. Chandrakant Singh, repulsing a counter-attack of infantry and tanks. Maj. Chandrakant earned an instant Vir Chakra for his brave leadership.

As a young Major, I was in command of 5 Independent Armoured Squadron (63 Cavalry), equipped with PT-76 tanks. In early November, the squadron had been ordered to assist the 61 Mountain Brigade in infiltrating behind Lalmai Hills in Comilla, 63 km west of Agartala. We had done all the reconnaissance and coordination to execute the operation, but after a change in plans on 28 November, the squadron was tasked to move with the infiltrating column with 4 Guards on the night of 1 December. We had no time to reconnoitre and to gather the terrain, and enemy obstacle layout along our route. It was therefore no surprise that on the night of our infiltration we were caught in a cleverly laid anti-tank ditch on the fringes of Akhaura. 4 Guards, ahead of us, was wading through deep slush. A ditch is no obstacle for the infantry, but for the tanks, it is designed to separate the infantry from the tanks.

After a night spent in recovery under intense enemy artillery fire, and faced with a relentless assault from the sky by the enemy Sabre jets the next morning, we recovered in time to assist 18 Rajput, commanded by the gallant Lt Col Ashok Verma, in a successful day attack on the enemy defences guarding the Akhaura railway station. Earlier, in a masterful frontal closing-in operation by 10 Bihar, commanded by the ever-cheerful Lt Col PC Sawhney—with lethal fire support provided by 65 Mountain Regiment, ably led by Col DS Bahl, and with the 57 Mountain Artillery Brigade fire support under Brig. Jangi Bawa—the enemy was pulverized. Attack by infiltration was an unorthodox plan. It worked. For us, the start could not have been more propitious.

Routed Pak brigade on the run

The momentous fall of Akhaura triggered a hasty retreat by Pakistan's 27 Infantry Brigade towards Meghna river, with India's tank squadron and 4 Guards in hot pursuit. Having captured the enemy advance defences at Talashahar, 4 Guards were ordered to break contact with the enemy and assemble at Brahmanbaria in anticipation of a new task, still under active consideration. Breaking contact with a withdrawing enemy in battle amounts to having the enemy on the ropes, yet not delivering the knockout punch. However, this is where experience and military judgement take over. At the tactical level, such a direction seemed strange; however, at the operational level, as it later turned out, the stage was being set for a bigger blow—Dhaka.

The 18 Rajput and 10 Bihar continued their relentless drive towards the bridge. This reinforced the enemy perception that our objective was to capture the bridge intact. Both battalions reached within 300 yards of the bridge on the Meghna. Such speed, always necessary when in contact with the enemy, is an adrenalin booster. So it was. However, the demolished bridges and culverts delayed the battalions' redeployment. Our troops were soon beyond the enemy's artillery range; besides, our Forward Air Controller, Flying Officer Shahid, had been injured, and his communication equipment destroyed.

With an SOS from 18 Rajput, my squadron detached from 4 Guards and joined the firefight. When we arrived, the battle was raging. The enemy brigade commander had launched a spoiling attack with infantry and tanks, supported by anti-tank guns. A melee ensued. My squadron lost three tanks in the firefight. One of them was led by my brave troop leader, Lt Rajindar Mohan, who was hit by an anti-tank gun after he had silenced two of the enemy's. He escaped with severe burn injuries. The enemy was neutralized by our joint action and their counter-attack fizzled out. Some Pakistani soldiers were killed, others escaped over the bridge, while a few got across on country boats. However, due to the ferocity of our pursuit, and to prevent the capture of the Meghna bridge, the Pakistani General in command of 14 Division, Maj. Gen. Majid, ordered its demolition. Commanders who leave their troops stranded across an obstacle and order its demolition tell the story of panic in the enemy garrison.

The masterstroke

With the bridge blown, our Corps Commander, Lt Gen. Sagat Singh, was at the proverbial dead end. History is replete with instances when in a battle situation there is an unanticipated pause—either because of one's own actions or the enemy's. The former gives you food for thought; the latter invariably provides you with a fleeting opportunity. Our General Officer Commanding (GOC) could have chosen to defer the advance and draw comfort from having completed his assigned task. However, Sagat's lifetime experience of combat told him otherwise. It served only to stoke the flame within him. For him, an opportunity beckoned. He had Dhaka in sight. He knew it was the strategic centre of gravity, the focal point—although it was beyond his brief. His experiences of the past intuitively brought a glint to his eye. He later described that day as the most exciting of his life. He could not let a brilliant opportunity go unaddressed. He knew what Dhaka meant in the larger scheme. He wagered on his intuition.

Sagat conferred with his Air Force commander, Group Captain Chandan Singh, and ordered a battalion to be flown in helicopters across the Meghna for the march to Dhaka—this later came to be known as the 'Helibridge over the Meghna'. The battalion was 4 Guards. There was some murmur about ground fire, to which Chandan retorted: 'I will be in the leading chopper.' That provided closure to the debate. The heli-lift of 4 Guards was Air Force's golden moment. The 110 Helicopter Unit, under Squadron Leader CS Sandhu's leadership, and supported by a band of brave young pilots, worked with precision and a tireless turnaround schedule. They positioned the battalion across the Meghna: a feat nonpareil.

Next, I was ordered to take my tanks across the Meghna. The Soviet-made PT-76 tank was designed to cross European rivers, which are generally 200–300 metres wide. In comparison, the Meghna was almost like a sea, and in the midst of the battle, and when ordered to cross it, to me it seemed like an ocean! I could not see the other bank. However, my GOC's intent was set in stone, and when he asked me whether we could cross the river, my reply was in the affirmative.

Having said that, I was not sure of the 'how' part of the operation. I was a greenhorn, and thank God for it! Greenhorns get smitten by commanders whose reputation and charisma settle for nothing less than the best. My answer had to be a 'Yes, sir'; and so it was. The speed of the water current in the

Meghna was in the double digits in knots. I don't know exactly
what it was, but I could see that the flow was very swift. As
the rivers get closer to the Bay of Bengal, they pick up speed
and the current is much stronger than what the PT-76 tanks
could negotiate in a near-perpendicular crossing across the
two banks, which is often the battle requirement when the
opposite bank is held. Fortunately, in our case, the far bank was
not held by the enemy. Anticipating that I would have to exit
downstream of my entry due to the speed of the water current,
I requested for a helicopter to do a reconnaissance of the river.
It was granted. Not satisfied with the first sortie, I asked for a
second sortie, and that, too, was approved. In the meantime,
my troop leader, Lt Raj Khindri, assisted by the locals, had
reconnoitred the home bank and found a marsh-free entry
route into the river. My aerial sorties helped me mark out small
islands in the river, which would allow me to make short hops.
The entry and exit points to the islands were laterally separated
by miles. My idea was to move from island to island—island
hopping, as it were. We hopped countless times and crossed.

Team India

The masterstroke of crossing the Meghna bypassing ground
opposition is a classic example of an operational manoeuvre
exercised by a military commander targeting the enemy mind. It
created 'shock and awe', a term that has now become fashionable
in the western capitals. The prospect of a captured Dhaka
galvanized everyone up and down the security establishment.
It saw Team India at its historic best. It led to the march of a
column, infantry, tanks and guns straight into the heart of the
centre of gravity. Further, as part of the teamwork in Delhi and

Kolkata, 2 Para, commanded by the daredevil Lt Col KS Pannu, was on standby to paradrop at Tangail, with a column of 1 Maratha under Lt Col KS 'Bulbul' Brar gliding down from Tura in Meghalaya for a link-up. The Navy was punishing Karachi with missiles from ships, accompanied by Petya-class frigates. The Indian Air Force, master of the skies in the east, having successfully flown an infantry battalion across the Meghna, was targeting the Government House at Dhaka, where Pakistani options to surrender or fight till the last were perhaps under discussion. At that stage we did not know which of the two options was finding favour. Leaflets were dropped over enemy emplacements exhorting Pakistani soldiers to surrender, lest they should fall into the hands of those they had tormented— the unfortunate Bengalis of East Pakistan.

Behind the scenes, the staff were busy—Maj Gen. Jacob in Kolkata was deliberating the Terms of Surrender. Lt Gen. Jagjit Aurora at his HQ in Kolkata, Lt Gen. Inder Gill, the Director General of Military Operations (DGMO), and Chief of the Army Staff (COAS) Gen. Sam Manekshaw were monitoring the battlefield and the developing global reactions. They were conscious that time was at a premium.

The intelligence agencies and the diplomats were tracking the Nixon–Kissinger threat of deploying the US 7th fleet in the Bay of Bengal. The trump card of the Indo-Soviet treaty, signed in August 1971, came into play, and India was supported with repeated vetoes by the Union of Soviet Socialist Republics (USSR) at the United Nations Security Council (UNSC). Our diplomats were also fighting Bhutto's canards at the UN. The administrators were gearing up for a temporary governance structure in the captured territory of East Pakistan till the Bangladeshis themselves took over. Prime Minister Indira

Gandhi and her colleagues held their nerves amidst intense rumours of intervention by the powers beyond.

This sort of seamless synergy is an assured recipe for success. There were tasks cut out and delivered on all fronts—military, diplomatic, political, strategic, operational and tactical. It is this synergy that enabled the capture of Dhaka after Sagat's breathtaking Meghna river-crossing manoeuvre. I learnt early in my service that initiative is not only a trait, but it is also a duty.

Mukti Bahini

In a matter of thirteen days, 75 million were rescued from possible genocide; it emphasized the totality of victory; 'shock and awe' with little or no collateral damage; a historical moment to be recorded in the archives of military history in India, and across the world. It was a lesson in the inextricable linkages between grand strategy and conflict-termination objectives. Unless the two are co-terminus, victory remains but a mirage.

In the fifty years since then, we have witnessed numerous military interventions where the absence of appropriate thought-out conflict-termination objectives has resulted in face-saving withdrawals. If Dhaka had not been addressed and its surrender not achieved, one more mirage would have been added to this ever-growing list.

The Mukti Bahini kept the wheel turning, keeping the momentum in our favour. In today's age, we talk about battlefield transparency rendered possible by sensors, radars, artificial intelligence and satellites. In 1971, battlefield transparency was, whenever possible, provided by the Mukti Bahini. Their presence and their will to fight for a just cause made an outstanding contribution towards the capitulation of the enemy before the Joint Command.

Indira Gandhi's statement in Parliament—'Dhaka is the free capital of a free country'—exemplifies twentieth century's most successful humanitarian intervention against genocide, surmounting all odds.

War Dispatches

Sidney Schanberg, the Pulitzer Prize-winning correspondent of *The New York Times* who rode into Dhaka with us, had this to say:

> I don't like sitting around praising armies. I don't like armies because armies mean wars. But this (Indian) army was something. They were great all the way. There never was a black mark ... I lived with the officers and I walked, rode with the jawans—and they were all great. Sure, some of them were scared at first—they wouldn't be human if they weren't. But I never saw a man flinch because he was scared. There was a tremendous spirit in the Indian Army and it did one good to experience it.

Lessons from a Maritime Success Story

Adm. Arun Prakash (Retd)

The Indian Navy was truly blooded during the Bangladesh war, in which an imaginative leadership boldly employed the full range of maritime capabilities; however, 1971 also brought to light some serious shortcomings

TO most sea-power advocates whose pleas, for decades, have been falling on deaf ears, it seemed ironic that the events of May 2020 in the icy Himalayan wastes should have focused the nation's attention on the maritime domain. To use a hackneyed idiom, chronic 'sea-blindness' among our decision-makers has been the bane of the Indian Navy (IN) and has served to stunt its growth since Independence. Even as our attention is currently engaged in predicting outcomes on our northern borders and in the waters of the Indo-Pacific, a look back at the 1971 Bangladesh conflict may be useful.

While the 1947 and 1962 conflicts had lacked a maritime dimension, the 1965 Indo-Pak war saw the IN discomfited by an unreasoned government directive not to initiate any offensive action at sea and not to permit its units north of Kathiawar. To add to the Navy's woes, a Pakistan Navy (PN) task force bombarded the coastal town of Dwarka and retired with impunity, leaving a psychological scar on the IN. However, just years later, the Indian subcontinent was again engulfed in a conflict, providing the IN a chance to vindicate itself.

In early 1971, Pakistan, riven by political and ethnic differences between its Punjabi-dominated western wing and its Bengali eastern wing, descended into civil war, triggering a massive exodus of East Pakistani refugees into India, thereby creating a social and economic crisis for India. The cynical American duo of President Nixon and his Chief of Staff, Henry Kissinger, not only lent full support to Pakistan's military rulers, but also egged on China to create military diversions for India. It was under these circumstances that Prime Minister Indira Gandhi, in consultation with her military commanders, crafted a grand strategy which would halt the Pakistan army's murderous rampage and reverse the refugee influx.

The IN, still smarting from the ignominy of inaction in 1965, ensured that it had an important role to play in the coming conflict. The Service was truly blooded during the Bangladesh war, in which an imaginative leadership boldly employed the full range of maritime capabilities.

While the heroic exploits of our sailors will be recounted elsewhere, here are a few defining events that not only encapsulated the significant maritime contribution to this conflict, but also highlighted some serious shortcomings of the IN:

• The deployment of small Soviet-built missile boats on the high seas and the use of radar-homing missiles, which devastated ships and shore targets in Karachi, were undoubtedly a demonstration of IN ingenuity and innovation.

• The sinking of merchant ships in Karachi, and the consequent stoppage of all shipping traffic to and from West Pakistan, highlighted the importance of trade warfare.

• The deployment of aircraft-carrier *INS Vikrant* to blockade East Pakistan was a gamble which paid off handsomely. *Vikrant's* air squadrons wreaked havoc on airfields, ports, harbours and riverine traffic in East Pakistan, expediting the surrender of Pakistani forces. This reinforced the Navy's faith in tactical air power; if a small carrier with an old aircraft could achieve this, ran the Navy reasoning, imagine what a bigger carrier could achieve.

• The sinking of PN submarine *Ghazi* off Visakhapatnam and the torpedoing of the frigate *INS Khukri* by *PNS Hangor* were both replete with lessons in submarine operations as well as in anti-submarine warfare (ASW) tactics.

• The fact that the 3,500-km transit of *PNS Ghazi* from Karachi to Visakhapatnam and the prolonged presence of *PNS Hangor* off our west coast remained undetected was a reflection on India's airborne ASW and maritime reconnaissance capabilities—so far the IAF's bailiwick.

• A botched landing of troops by tank landing ships near Cox's Bazar, a town on the southeast coast of Bangladesh, revealed grave shortcomings in Indian amphibious training and inter-Service cooperation. While a Chinese diversionary attack, despite active encouragement by Nixon, failed to materialize, actual intervention on behalf of Pakistan came from an unexpected quarter: the USA. A task force led by nuclear carrier *USS Enterprise* entered the Bay of Bengal to warn India off West Pakistan. It turned out to be a futile gesture but provided a lesson to India in coercive realpolitik, reinforcing the case for strong sea-denial capability for India to insulate itself against foreign interference.

This war saw the IN employing the full gamut of its maritime capabilities, including missile warfare, carrier operations, submarine and anti-submarine warfare, trade warfare, amphibious operations, shore bombardment, special operations and mine counter-measures. It was fondly hoped that the IN contribution to the 1971 victory would stamp, indelibly, on the minds of India's decision-makers the vital role that maritime power could play in India's security matrix. That this did not happen has been amply demonstrated by the Navy's dwindling share in the defence budget over the past fifty years.

The nature of warfare has, no doubt, transformed since 1971. However, given the reality that the growing Chinese military pressure in the north, coupled with a steady naval build-up in the Indo-Pacific, could have ominous security implications for India, perhaps some lessons of the past will be useful.

Rule of Law vs Rule by 'Strong' Leader

Rajesh Ramachandran

Lessons India needs to learn in the golden jubilee year of the Bangladesh liberation

FIFTY years is almost a lifetime, and the right time-span to look back on an event, particularly if the golden jubilee is that of a spectacular, unparalleled modern military victory. A poor nation of hungry millions standing up to a warring sibling founded, armed and funded by a former Empire and a modern superpower, and yet achieving a stupendous victory against all odds is a chapter of history that we need to read many times over. With a Parsi Chief of Army Staff, Sikh and Jewish generals, a Muslim Assistant Chief of Air Staff, and a predominantly

Hindu force, India's army was a professional one that brought about the 1971 victory. It was an army completely oblivious to identity politics and its sinister sectarian manipulations. Every arm of the fledgling Indian state, be it spymaster RN Kao's boys or the Border Security Force men and officers under KF Rustamji, worked like cogs in a big wheel which relentlessly rolled on, crushing the enemy's genocidal, communal army, tearing Pakistan into two, redrawing the blood-soaked colonial map left behind by the retreating Empire, and rewriting the sad story of subcontinental fratricide.

Can we repeat the 1971 victory now? How many among the heroes of 1971 would have even chosen to remain in present-day India? For instance, the Royal Air Force's ace pilot Idris Hasan Latif had rejected Jinnah's Pakistan to choose Gandhi's India; but would he do it all over again, in an atmosphere filled with fear of the unknown National Register of Citizens? And what about Sam Manekshaw, JFR Jacob and Rustamji? Would they have preferred a more cosmopolitan London or New York or Melbourne to a strife-torn Indian city where youngsters remain anxious about their identity and farmers fight for their survival? These are important questions that should be asked in the fiftieth year of the Bangladesh liberation war.

Another great lesson of the 1971 war was that it was fought after a general election and not before or for an election. Indira Gandhi had won the Lok Sabha elections conclusively in March 1971, winning 352 seats out of the 518 seats that went to polls. She had initially wanted the attack in April, but was turned down by the army—an instance of a no-nonsense military leadership and a listening political headship. The military planned, executed and won the war, and when Dhaka fell in December, neither Indira nor Manekshaw flew in for a photo-op. It was left to the deserving Eastern Command Chief to do the needful. Thus, a new nation was born, which in its fiftieth year of founding stands tall and firm.

But India faced its biggest setback as a nation and as a democracy thereafter. The very same leader who had let the military and the bureaucracy do their job and had refused to make political capital out of the moment of military triumph soon metamorphosed into a dictator, imprisoning Opposition leaders, imposing censorship, letting her son rule by proxy, and postponing elections. So, is Indira's makeover the real lesson of the 1971 victory—the emergence of a strong leader in an institutionally weak country? As a leader who changed the international map, creating a nation and annexing new territory (Sikkim), Indira remains without parallel in our nation, but she also took the nation into dictatorship and made us aware of how fragile our democratic institutions are.

India craves strong leaders—in election after election this is in evidence. From Indira to LK Advani to Narendra Modi, we have had politicians trying to plug into this current of national yearning. Some of them succeeded and many failed. Yet, we refuse to acknowledge this sentiment, which often is mistaken for right-wing nationalism. A strong leader is the people's cure for weak institutions of the functioning Indian chaos. The stronger the messaging about the messiah, the more receptive the voters are for deliverance. Whether the promise is of politically neutral development heralding prosperity through jobs and greater income, or of a tougher national security state taking on enemies, real or imaginary, voters seek out strong leaders who are seemingly in control. Of course, strong leaders have been defeated in the past when their messaging lost credibility, the best examples being the personal defeats of

Indira and Sanjay, along with the defeat of their party, in 1977. Yet, the chaotic Janata experiment that followed only ended in the people turning to their tried and tested strong leader.

September 2021 marked seventy-five years since the first interim government headed by Nehru took over the reins of governance to give India the rule of law. Yet, India still believes in the myth of rule by a leader. This belief, though it is almost akin to the worshipful wait for the next avatar, cannot be dismissed as a pre-modern society's superstitious angst. Had it been so, Indira would not have been voted out of power. The desire for the strong leader is a legitimate need for order—the quest for a super-arching authority to put the brute queue-jumpers in place, to create a more just society for the meek. This wish is probably because of our deep insecurity, stemming from our inability to manage our own resources in small groups. The feudal hierarchy of the villages cannot be solely blamed for this inability, for it is replicated in big cities that do not necessarily care for caste or communal pecking orders.

Indira succeeded in 1971 because she inherited a system that was still largely new in terms of its organizational integrity and was idealistic in its intent. It was just twenty-three years after the Mahatma's assassination, and there was plenty of idealism in the air. But the present-day strong leaders need to analyse whether they can repeat Indira's feat while presiding over a people anxious about discord and dissension within the nation.

Coming of Age in a Two-Front War

Air Vice Marshal Arjun Subramaniam (Retd)

The IAF showcased its prowess in tactical, operational, strategic domains; orchestrating the air battle involved six months of careful planning

WHILE the IAF operated in the 1947–48 and 1965 wars with Pakistan primarily in a tactical and supporting role to the Army, the 1971 two-front war saw the IAF showcase its prowess in roles and missions that straddled the tactical, operational and strategic domains.

At the heart of this newly found confidence was a systematic build-up of capability in areas other than the mere acquisition or upgradation of aerial platforms. The Russians and the ordnance factories were pushed to deliver adequate stocks of weapons; new airfields sprung up, and infrastructure, like protective aircraft shelters (blast pens), were built in several frontline airfields to ensure that the IAF was not caught napping during a pre-emptive strike, as it was in 1965. Reinforcing air defence in both the eastern and the western sectors was a chain of radars and mobile observation posts (MOPs) that provided an additional layer of early warning. IAF fighter pilots had benefited immensely from the formation of the Tactics and Combat Development Establishment (TACDE); the transport fleet had expanded its roles to include bombing and airborne operations; and finally, the helicopter fleet had gathered significant operational experience in Nagaland and Mizoram in specialized heli-borne operations that paid rich dividends during the 'Lightning Campaign' that unfolded in East Pakistan.

On the covert front, in late September 1971, Air Chief Marshal Pratap Chunder Lal, himself a Bengali, was instrumental in assigning a base and gifting a few aircraft with instructors to Kilo Force, as the fledgling Bangladesh Air Force came to be known. Operating out of a small airstrip in Dimapur in Nagaland, Kilo Force was commanded by Group Captain AK Khandker, who later became the first Chief of the Bangladesh Air Force. It had on its inventory a Dakota freighter aircraft, an Otter light transport aircraft and an Alouette helicopter. The Otter and Alouette were suitably modified to fire rockets and guns and took part in ground support operations during the conflict.

Even as the Indian Army was shaping the battlefield on the eastern front prior to commencement of hostilities on the western front, the IAF drew first blood in a remarkable aerial dogfight over Boyra Salient, located in the north-west part of East Pakistan, on 22 November, when Pakistan Air Force (PAF) Sabres attempted to strafe Indian infantry units as they established pivots for further advance. Scrambled from Dum Dum airfield in Kolkata, four Gnat fighters of the 22 Squadron took down two F-86 Sabre jets and earned the IAF its first three Vir Chakras.

The initial days of the air war in the east saw two major objectives being achieved by the IAF. The first was effective neutralization of the lone Sabre squadron in East Pakistan by repeatedly attacking the Tejgaon airfield outside Dacca till it was unusable. Though the IAF suffered attrition during the first few days, both to Sabres and to ground fire, it achieved almost total air superiority by 7 December, thus paving the way for unrestricted close air support (CAS) as well as heli-borne and airborne operations.

The second objective achieved was effective CAS at some of the tough ground battles being fought at the border posts of Hilli, Kamalpur and Akhaura, besides the Belonia bulge, a small enclave in southeastern Bangladesh that protruded into the Indian state of Tripura. The one significant difference in this war, as compared to the 1965 one, was that every corps had a tactical air centre (TAC) with trained forward air controllers (FACs) who orchestrated CAS in response to the requirements of the field commanders. The overwhelming superiority of numbers meant that the IAF also concurrently carried out interdiction of trains, ammo dumps and defences around the fortresses of Dacca, Narayanganj and Sylhet. This was done primarily by the rocket-firing Hunters and Sukhoi-7s as they blasted logistics reinforcements and defences around the beleaguered garrisons.

A major heli-borne operation was conducted on 7 December as the entire 4th battalion of 5 Gorkha Rifles was landed close to Sylhet Garrison by the 105 Helicopter Unit and was supported by a couple of armed Mi-4 helicopters. If the heli-borne operation at Sylhet was a heavyweight boxer's right hook, 4 Corps Commander Lt Gen. Sagat Singh's heli-lifting of a brigade's worth of troops between 9 and 11 December across the mighty river Meghna to two landing zones at Raipura and Narsingdi, barely 60 km from Dacca, was a solid punch to Gen. AAK Niazi's gut. Not satisfied with that, Lt Gen. Sagat Singh pressed on with a left hook on 12 December, heli-lifting another brigade to Narayanganj, around 40 km south-east of Dacca. Between 6 and 12 December, a fourteen-helicopter task force from three units (105, 110 and 111 Helicopter Units) had landed over 4,000 troops, and most of their supporting equipment, including ammunition and light artillery guns, in three locations in East Pakistan, by flying around 350 sorties, including over 100 by night—a truly spectacular effort.

The Tangail para-drop operation by the 2 Para on 11 December in the area to the north of Dacca involved over fifty transport aircraft along with Gnat and MiG-21 fighter escorts. The operation fulfilled its objectives of coercing Gen. Niazi to surrender as it caused panic in Dacca with news trickling in that a brigade had been dropped and that it was only a matter of time before the forces converged on Dacca.

The psychological impact of innovative operations generally gets underplayed in any post-war analysis. One such operation that caused a disproportionate impact on the psyche of East Pakistan's leadership as they huddled in Dacca during the closing stages of the war was the strike by IAF fighters on the Governor's House on 14 December. In an operation driven by hard intelligence based on wireless intercepts, four MiG-21s and four Hunters attacked the palatial house in the vicinity of Dacca Cricket Stadium in quick succession while Governor

Malik himself was chairing a meeting with UN officials in attendance. MiG-21s from 28 Squadron followed up with rocket attacks on specific buildings in Dacca University where suspected Pakistani troops and collaborators were taking shelter.

Air power delivered disproportionate effects in the battle for Bangladesh and hastened the surrender of 93,000 able-bodied troops of the Pakistan army as they wilted in the face of a combined assault by Indian soldiers, sailors and airmen. Orchestrating the air battle was not an easy task and involved over six months of careful planning and strategizing to first create an overwhelming superiority, and then drive home the advantage to achieve decisive operational outcomes.

Exploits in the Western Sector

Air Vice Marshal Arjun Subramaniam (Retd)

Though it was not able to achieve complete air superiority, the IAF inflicted greater attrition on the PAF in 1971 as compared to 1965

O N the western borders, the IAF had over 350 fighters and bombers available for full-fledged operations, considering that all squadrons had been asked to ensure a serviceability of 75 per cent at the very minimum. These included over four squadrons of MiG-21s with the innovatively added external gun pack, upgraded Hunters, Gnats, the recently acquired Soviet Sukhoi-7s, HAL-built HF-24s, Mysteres, Canberra bombers and the obsolescent Vampire jets, which would go on to play an important role in the J&K sector. Facing them were 260–280 PAF fighters and bombers, including a squadron of twenty-four newly acquired Mirage-IIIs from France; barely a squadron of ageing F-104 Starfighters, reinforced by an additional ten from the Royal Jordanian Air Force; and around seven squadrons of the battle-hardened Sabre jets. These included ninety upgraded Sabres from the German Air Force through the good offices of the Shah of Iran. One squadron of B-57 bombers and five squadrons of the Chinese variant of the MiG-19, the F-6—gifted to Pakistan by China in 1966—made up the remaining force.

What was significant in the steady build-up of IAF capability was that its chief, Air Chief Marshal Lal, had a ringside view of all the mistakes made during the 1965 war—he had been the Vice Chief during that period. In his quiet and unassuming way, Lal went about addressing the major deficiencies using a systems approach. His strategy vis-à-vis Pakistan prior to the 1971 war was simple: build asymmetry by widening both the qualitative and quantitative gaps between the two air forces.

While the Gnats continued to dominate the Sabres, the enhanced ground-attack punch provided by the upgraded Hunters and the relatively new Sukhoi-7s gave the IAF a decisive qualitative and quantitative advantage. Most importantly, the coercive impact of the MiG-21s in the air defence role meant that the PAF was not going to have a free run as it attacked IAF airfields and other ground targets. While in 1965 the IAF was somewhat surprised by PAF tactics, it was better prepared in 1971. An example of this was the 'defensive split' air combat tactics of the PAF, in which the Sabres, when 'bounced', would split to give themselves a chance of engaging the two attacking Gnats in two separate 1-vs-1s, thereby neutralizing the initial advantage of the attackers. If the Gnats did not split, the free Sabre would then manoeuvre offensively to get behind the trail

Gnat. In 1971, none of this happened as the Gnats were always game to take on the Sabres in a one-vs-one. The enhanced range of the Hunters meant that all PAF airfields were within their radius of action. The IAF had also trained for low-level bombing by night in moonlight conditions with a motley bunch of MiG-21 and Sukhoi-7 pilots from the recently formed Tactics and Combat Development Establishment, putting together Standard Operating Procedures for 'blind bombing' in limited moonlight conditions—this was to pay rich dividends during the initial days of the air campaign in the western sector.

The raids on IAF airfields and installations on the evening of 3 December and early morning of 4 December were spread across the western front. Srinagar and its satellite air base of Avantipur in the J&K sector, Pathankot, Amritsar, Halwara, Ambala and Sirsa airfields in the Punjab sector, and Bikaner, Jaisalmer, Jodhpur and Uttarlai in the Rajasthan sector, were all attacked by fighter and bomber aircraft of the PAF. However, poor planning, inadequate force levels (barely thirty-five to forty were flown in the first strike), poor execution and a robust IAF air defence resulted in a negligible impact on the operational potential of the IAF to respond, which it did with measured professionalism the next day.

Hoping to draw the IAF towards Sargodha in large retaliatory strikes, the PAF was surprised that the IAF chose to respond by carrying out limited strikes through the day and night with their all-weather day/night-capable fighter bombers, the Sukhoi-7 and the dependable Hunters, with Canberra bombers and MiG-21s keeping up the pressure by night. MiG-21s and Gnats provided effective top cover to ground attack missions and ensured that the IAF managed to keep attrition down in the first few days. Here, too, having seen the debilitating impact of the opening days of the 1965 air war on IAF morale, Lal had realized that it was important to keep attrition down at the commencement of hostilities.

Not widely known is that hours after the PAF struck several IAF airfields in the western sector on the evening of 3 December, the most unlikely of bombing platforms, An-12s from 44 Squadron, bombed a well-concealed armament and logistics depot south-west of Lahore in the Changa Manga forest. The An-12 squadron, brilliantly led by Wing Commander Vashisht, went on to attack the Sui gas plant, a corps headquarters near Bahawalpur, and an artillery brigade near the Haji Pir Pass, a strategically located mountain pass in Pakistan-occupied Kashmir (PoK) on the Pir Panjal Ranges. Vashisht also led a daring raid along with Canberra bombers over Skardu, a PAF base located north of the Kashmir Valley in the Gilgit-Baltistan region of PoK. The IAF gradually established a steady ascendancy over the PAF and even delivered a decisive punch on Pakistani armour in the historic battle of Longewala, where Hunters from Jaisalmer pounded Pakistan's 18 Division to submission, and forced it to abandon its offensive in the desert sector. Among the other early accomplishments were effective attacks by Hunter fighter bombers and Canberra bombers on the Kiamari oil refineries, the Masroor airfield and the harbour at Karachi, which coincided with the Indian Navy's daring missile boat attacks on Karachi Port and the Pakistani Navy on the nights of 4 and 8 December. Rounding off the exploits, and unmindful of the grave danger of scrambling and taking off even as an air raid was in progress over Srinagar airfield, Flying Officer Nirmaljit Singh Sekhon shot down one Sabre jet and badly damaged another before he himself was shot down in the dogfight where he was outnumbered four to one.

The intensity and scope of air operations in the western sector far exceeded that on the eastern front. With near parity in the western sector, the IAF flew more than twice the number of sorties as compared to 1965, and though it was not able to achieve complete air superiority, it inflicted greater attrition on the PAF as compared to 1965 and prevented it from operating to its full potential. Though Lal had articulated a departure from old aerial strategies, the offensive flavour of strikes on several strategic targets certainly had an impact on the Pakistani mindset and demonstrated India's willingness to strike deep to hurt an adversary's economic potential.

A Rare Honour: Born to Battle

Lt Gen. Raj Sujlana (Retd)

A 1971 war veteran remembers his days at the NDA and the IMA

DESTINY came calling in the summer of 1967; July of the year saw around 250 of us in our mid-teens or a little older converge from all parts of the country in the salubrious environs of Khadakwasla to join the crucible of military leadership, the National Defence Academy (NDA). We had heard what it was like for beginners at the Academy, but still, what confronted us was an environment we could never have imagined. Our looks were the first to change, all minus the turbaned underwent a drastic transformation after their first 'Mess Tin' hair cut! The rumble-tumble of the Academy was tough, but as the days passed, an unannounced bond built up among us, and great camaraderie and lifelong friendships came about. We cheered each other to move on; no favours were sought, but our togetherness, team spirit and tenacity grew. We toughened physically and mentally, persevered in our progress, and acclimatized to the new life to pass the training years in good cheer.

The last six months of training were specific to the service we were to join. The future sailors headed for Peacock Bay to feel the wind in their sails, the wannabe pilots for the glider drome, and we the army guys—'Pongos', as all called us fondly—slipped into dungarees and remained grounded. We learnt the first important lessons; *'Ek Goli Ek Dushman'* and the skill of bayonet fighting, the cutting edge of victory through the centuries. The flash of the bayonet added to our daring and gusto, and blood literally rose to our faces when we charged the dummy targets; in later years, with the regimental war cry added, it made for a deadly cocktail. It was the enemy or me, and we were ready for the famous words, *'Sir, if that be so, we will get them with the bayonet!'* Our instructors left lasting impressions on us, the inimitable Academy Adjutant, Maj. Soli Canteenwala, Subedar Maj. Kanshi Ram, and many others.

Fast-forward to 6 June 1970: three years were behind us as we stood on the drill square. 'We had come in as raw boys and were passing out as hardened men.' As we slow-marched, our inter-Service togetherness was on display; we saluted the quarter deck, the overhead air force jets dipped in salute, with the junior-most course at the NDA on the ladders, shouting *'38th Course Ki Jai!'* After the first leg of our training, a short relaxing break and we headed for the service-specific institutions for the final leg of our training before being commissioned. The Navy cadets joined Training Ship *TIR*, the Air Force cadets reported

to Bidar, and the Army cadets headed for the Indian Military
Academy, Dehradun (IMA). At IMA, cadets joining through
the Direct Entry, Army Cadet College and Technical streams
became an integral part of us, the 47th Regular Course.

Our momentous commissioning

One year at the IMA flashed by, bringing four years of rigorous
toil to an end. In the early 1970s, the strength of a passing-out
course batch was smaller, and it was possible to conduct the
pipping ceremony within the precincts of the august Chetwode
Hall. For every future officer, Chetwode Hall has an esteemed
place in their hearts. Engraved there is the credo they must
follow: '*The Safety, Honour and Welfare of your country come
first, Always and Every Time. The Honour, Welfare, and Comfort
of the men you Command come next. Your own Ease, Comfort
and Safety come last, Always and Every Time*'.

On 12 June 1971, dressed in 'White Patrols', the summer
ceremonial dress, we assembled in the Hall under the shadow
of portraits of former Army Chiefs, IMA Commandants
and the gallantry award winners, and awaited the stroke of
midnight. Our heart beats quickened as darkness engulfed us;
brightness followed with the band playing 'Congratulations'.
Our near and dear ones were close at hand, the cover over
the stars was unveiled by parents and siblings, and the Hall
was filled with a sea of sparkling stars. Dancing followed;
partners or no partners, it was a time for everyone to savour
and kick up. The unforgettable night had to close as the
parade awaited us on the morrow, but every moment remains
etched in our minds.

Early in the morning on 13 June, we were in the drill square facing the historic Chetwode building; the façade seemed to beckon us to pass through its folds. Dark low clouds hovered overhead and a heavy downpour caught us square; we took it as a blessing of the Almighty. Totally drenched, the cottons stuck to our skin and the hackles swayed on the headgear, but we stood sentinel-like, unshakeable—nothing could take this moment away from us. The Parade got underway as the sharpness of commands of Dimpy Bhardwaj, the Sword of Honour recipient, echoed through the drill square. With our best foot forward, heels digging in, arms swinging in unison, our columns moved meticulously past the Reviewing Officer (RO), presenting our swords and eyes right in salute. We were cheered by our proud parents, siblings and friends. Our morale was sky high when we heard the RO compliment our immaculate smartness, perfect drill and rare gusto despite the inclement weather. The grand finale arrived, and the haunting strains of 'Auld Lang Syne' filled the air as we slow-marched for the final journey towards the hallowed portals of the Chetwode Building. The 'Antim Pag' awaited us. As we stepped into the portals, we crossed the rubicon; from Gentlemen Cadets we became Gentlemen Officers of the great Indian Army. Our pride was boundless as we cheered ourselves dressed in our respective regimental accoutrements. Farewells followed, and we departed with cherished memories, little realizing that for some this would be their last such meeting.

After our short holiday, by the first week of July, it was time to bid 'Au Revoir' to our families. We were excited no end but the goodbyes were somewhat teary, the words of Richard Le Gallienne unsaid but reflecting clearly the thoughts of our parents, '*Soldier going to war—will you take my heart with you, so that I may share a little in the famous things you do? Soldier going to war—If in battle you must fall, will you, among the faces, see my face the last of all?*' War was in our destiny; we have the distinction of being part of the first course batch which, on passing out, went straight to battle. War experience for any soldier, sailor or airman is the ultimate; yes, there is a cost, comrades will be lost, some incapacitated, but then, that is part of soldiering. We were lucky to gain war experience as active participants in the 1971 Indo-Pak war, which led to the liberation of Bangladesh.

Most of us reported to our respective units already at their battle stations. Some who joined units in the east drove straight into active hostilities. We were privileged to earn our spurs under the shadow of and in the war. We learnt at every step, observed the hectic planning and build-up underway. Intermingling with our soldiers gave us tremendous confidence. They were the best we could get, dedicated to the core, sure of victory and ready to lay down their lives—and so were we! Some of our batchmates never returned from the bloody battles. They died honourable deaths, and not before conveying to the enemy that '*Veerta ki jaan hain (hum), Bharat ki shaan hain, tere hi kachar mein, tujhe ki hila diya* (Valour is in our blood, we are India's pride, we rattled you in your own backyard).' We rightly earned the sobriquet of 'Born to Battle!' It may sound odd to mention a little-known fact: in those non-digitized days, the first pay came after three or four months of service. Sadly, those from our course who lost their lives in the war never got an opportunity to spend even a paisa of their earnings—'*They didn't seek fame or money; they only sought the glory of the Tricolour!*' With honour, their names are daubed in golden letters in the sacred space at the Hut of Remembrance at NDA and in the War Memorial at the IMA, our alma mater.

Of the many brave acts performed by the Born to Battle officers in the war and in subsequent years, a few are recounted here. The 9 Para Special Forces were at Poonch on 4–5 December; 2/Lt (later Maj. Gen.) Ashok Taskar, 'Tusky' to us, was rushed forward to block an infiltrating enemy column. He did this successfully, as he says, 'with the blessings of Nagali Gurdwara'. An assault by his Group Commander came from another direction and, sandwiched between the two, the enemy had no escape. Forty-one of them lay dead. Tusky was awarded the Sena Medal for bravery. Again, on the night of 13–14 December, six officers with 120 men, divided into seven assault teams (one under Tusky), successfully raided the enemy gun position 15 to 17 km inside Pakistan territory near Mandhol village, south-west of Poonch. After an intense hand-to-hand fight, sixty enemy troops were killed and six 122-mm Chinese-origin guns were blasted. We lost two men with twelve wounded. But true to the words 'Leave no one behind', all were carried back home for last rights and amelioration. It was a true surgical strike, decades before the current noise about a similar operation.

The 16th of December, the Battle of Basantar. Poona Horse was advancing and one of its squadrons got involved in a sharp tank engagement. The enemy force was large and reinforcements were called for. 2/Lt Arun Khetarpal close by quickly responded. He came leading his troop of tanks and an encounter followed. Ten enemy tanks lay burning. Not satisfied with this, Arun moved for further kills, but his tank was hit and it burst into flames. When asked to abandon the tank, he replied, '*No sir, I will not abandon my tank. My main gun is still working!'* He continued his battle till his last breath. He was honoured with the Param Vir Chakra, posthumously. The enemy acknowledged his valiance. In the words of Pakistani Brigadier KM Naser, *'Arun's courage was exemplary, he moved his tank with fearless courage and daring ... he stood like an unsurmountable rock, between victory and defeat, of the counter-attack by Pak 13 Lancers on Dec 16.'*

Just the previous day, Tom Bakshi (later Maj. Gen.), another course mate of Khetarpal's, had fondly recounted how unhesitatingly Khetarpal, with his tank, had winched out his vehicle stuck in the quagmire. Bakshi later earned the Sena Medal in counter-terrorist operations.

Our batchmates in the Navy went to war as Midshipmen, on board various frigates, destroyers and high-speed patrol boats. They experienced the thrill of fearlessly prowling the seas despite the threat of the US 7th Fleet. The ones on small high-speed boats were tasked with the defence of the coastline and the ports. Two of our lot were deputed on *INS Khukri*, which sailed out on 9 December for a search-and-destroy mission in the Bay of Bengal. The *Khukri* was torpedoed by *PNS Hangor*, a Pakistan submarine. True to the highest naval tradition, Captain MN Mulla, along with eighteen officers (including our Midshipman AG Patil) and a crew of 178 sailors, went down with the ship. Our air warriors were raring to go. As war broke out, all instructors and aircraft were moved forward for operational duty, because of which their final stage of getting wings on their chest was postponed to January 1972. During service, they had displayed top-grade proficiency in combat flying; TS Randhawa (later Air Marshal), for long, was part of and later the leader of the aerial acrobatics team of 'Thunderbolts'.

Bravery remained our forte. There can be no better example of this than Col NJC Nair, who in two outstanding operations was decorated first with the Kirti Chakra and then the Ashok Chakra (posthumously), the two highest gallantry awards for peacetime soldiering. And then there was Sumit Mukherjee (later Air Marshal), whose aircraft suffered a serious bird hit, but who, despite extreme danger to his life, landed his fighter safely and was awarded the Shaurya Chakra.

On the professional side, nearly seventy of us obtained the flag ranks, which included a score of three stars. Among our Air Force buddies from the first course, five went on to become Air Marshals—some record to beat! Many batchmates left early and ventured into other fields successfully. The most outstanding example of this was the making of aviation history by the pioneering budget airline in India, Air Deccan. This was also an example of our continued bonds. Four of our artillery batchmates—Capt. GR Gopinath, Samuel, Poovaiah and Rawal—had joined hands in this venture. Coincidently, all other than Gopinath were high-grade pilots.

A reunion we missed

The 13th of June 2021 marked fifty years of our passing out from IMA. We were all looking forward to returning to the Academy to celebrate our Golden Jubilee, to reminisce, to laugh, to share pranks and stories of the past. Our camaraderie had never diminished and it needed no reignition, but a gathering is always rejuvenating. Most importantly, it is an occasion to remember those who have gone to the yonder world but still remain with us in spirit. The pandemic, however, put paid to this. Our physical meet had to be dropped and we turned to the new norm of the webinar.

Our meet started with a remembrance for our stars; the last post was sounded and their names scrolled. Their spirit was definitely among us. It reminded us of the words in 'From the Fallen': *'They shall not grow old, as we that are left; age shall not weary them nor the years condemn, at the going down of the sun and in the morning, we will remember them always.'*

Our exuberance to meet was evident in the webinar open session, where everyone reached out to everyone else. It was cross-talk galore and we felt our oneness, though we were so far from each other. We were Babuas, Bongs, Kanchas, Mizos, Punjies, Sirdies, Tants, Thambis ... but all as close-knit as ever. Course get-togethers have always been events to look forward to; I had the privilege to host one as Commandant, IMA a decade back. I had superannuated from IMA, and it was nostalgic to be ridden out of the Mukhya Dwar to bid farewell to arms in the Commandant's four-horse buggy. I left with these thoughts:

> Where else would we have got such a satisfying profession to lead men who stood tall in every adversity and taught us to battle; gave us unbeatable comradeship of nearly 400 lifelong friends and wonderful ladies who stood by us through thick and thin and will stand by each other till the last call.

Our association has a special flavour—to quote Gulzar, *'Kuch rishton mein munafa nahi hota, par zindagi ko amir bana dete hain*! (some relationships are not profitable, but they enrich life!)'

The Western Sector: A Saga of Valour and Failures

Manoj Joshi

In the east, India won the war it could not have lost; in the west,
however, it did not exactly succeed—the lessons are many

THE victory of the Indian Army that led to the creation of
Bangladesh in 1971 was a splendid achievement. Like all
wars, things did not go according to plan, but the generals, in
particular, Lt Gen. Sagat Singh and Maj. Gen. JFR Jacob, were
able to quickly adapt to the developing situation and the war
was brought to a close in quick time. The huge Pakistani army
had to meekly surrender without a real fight. But the same
cannot be said of the fighting in the western sector, where, to
put it simply, the Indian Army failed.

In the east, India won the war, which it could not have lost. So, the real challenge was in the west, where there was a rough parity between the two sides. To an extent, the Indians handicapped themselves by the political directions that called for maintaining a defensive posture till the Pakistanis revealed their hand. But once war broke out, bad general-ship, poor plans, indifferent execution and dogged defence by the Pakistanis became the norm. History should provide an important corrective to those who think that India can steamroll Pakistan in the event of a war—and one must learn from it.

Jammu & Kashmir

The one big success in the west came from a more-or-less unplanned local operation launched at the instance of Maj. Chewang Rinchen, Commander of Ladakh Scouts, which comprised four companies (around 400 men). They handled both the Chinese and Pakistani threats in the Nubra valley. Beginning with the capture of a high feature overlooking the Pakistani part of the Shyok valley, Rinchen rapidly captured the Chalunka mountain complex. The Pakistani Karakoram Scouts resisted, but they were overwhelmed. The small Indian force captured Turtuk, and by December 17, had advanced to Thang.

Some 800 sq. km of territory was captured. Maj. Rinchen got a Bar to his MVC earned in 1947-48. The territory gained has been invaluable for the defence of the Siachen area subsequently.

Had the operation been properly planned, there is no reason why Indian forces could not have reached the confluence of the Shyok and the Indus. It could have worked well with another operation that had been launched to capture Pakistani positions in Kargil. These posts had been captured twice and returned to Pakistan in 1965. They overlooked the Srinagar–Leh highway, and the local commanders had decided to capture them again in 1971. But the Pakistanis had by now fortified their approaches well and the Indian offensive up the Shingo river found the going tough. By the time of the ceasefire, some thirty-five posts out of about eighty had been captured by the Indian Army. Casualties were heavy, especially cases of frostbite.

At the time of the ceasefire in 1947–48, the Pakistanis were at Burzil Pass, but they surreptitiously came forward after the ceasefire and occupied posts overlooking Kargil, requiring repeated action by India. A look at the map would have suggested a better-supported operation that could have pushed the Pakistani forces back 20–30 km into Gilgit–Baltistan, an action that would have prevented the Kargil war.

The 19 Division operations in the Kashmir valley had only limited success. In the Lipa valley, the division claimed they had captured 150 sq. km, but the Pakistanis infiltrated back and forced the Indians out in March 1972.

In Poonch, India won an excellent defensive victory by foiling a Pakistani plan to capture the town and all the area up to Pir Panjal. To capitalize on the Pakistani failure the Indian side decided to improve its defensive positions, but the ambitious operation to secure Daruchian failed because of poor handling of the forces.

Finally, India suffered a big loss in the capture of Chhamb by Pakistani forces. This was, in many ways, a repetition of 1965.

Punjab

The story was more or less the same down the international border to Kutch. There were important local victories, such as the capture of Chicken's Neck and outstanding bravery all around, but a breakthrough eluded the Indian Army. There were also setbacks in Hussainiwala and Fazilka.

A lot of Indian opinion on the battle of the Shakargarh bulge is tinged with tales of valour, especially that of 2nd Lt Arun Khetarpal, PVC. But in terms of what India put in and what it got out of the operation, there is little doubt that it was a failure.

The Pakistani defences were deep, and the offensive by 1 Corps soon got bogged down in clearing them. The Indian force was unable to achieve even its initial objectives. The principal Indian objective had been the capture of the Shakargarh bulge which included the towns of Shakargarh and Zafarwal. But by the end of the war, India had neither been able to breach the Pakistani chain of defences comprising Zafarwal and Dhamtal–Narowal, nor had it captured Shakargarh. As the official history says, 'The failures only added regrettable chapters to a ponderous story of excessive caution and no ingenuity.'

Rajasthan

The average person's recall of the Rajasthan leg of the war comes from the movie *Border* and the gallant defence of the area by Maj. Chandpuri. But this was well inside the Indian territory and, had Pakistani plans succeeded, they would have indeed been breakfasting at the Jaisalmer air base. Instead, as soon as the Indian Air Force (IAF) heard of the Longewala battle, it decimated the Pakistani tanks. India's failure was in not detecting the Pakistani build-up and then in not mounting a counter-offensive and capturing Rahim Yar Khan in Sindh.

Both India and Pakistan planned offensives here, virtually parallel to each other, but neither side was aware of the other's plans until they actually unfolded. Both offensives got underway on the morning of 5 December. The Pakistani offensive aimed at Jaisalmer got bogged down in Longewala. But as the threat suddenly emerged in Longewala, the Indian offensive to Rahim Yar Khan was postponed. This switch of the mission delayed the pursuit of the retreating Pakistanis and, in the end, the Indian troops failed to resume their advance towards Rahim Yar Khan.

Conclusion

The Western Army Commander, Lt Gen. KP Candeth, claimed that the task of his army was 'to hold the enemy at bay, while Eastern Command overran East Pakistan'. It was not as though offensive tactics were not deployed in the western sector. It is just that they failed. As military historian Maj. Gen. Sukhwant Singh put it, 'Candeth and his Generals come out the worst. They had no concept of conducting a short war. They dissipated their efforts in outmoded World War II ideas.'

1971 is a cautionary tale for those ready to declare war on Pakistan at the drop of a hat.

The Visionary Warrior Sagat Singh

Maj. Gen. Randhir Sinh (Retd)

Celebrating the leadership, heroism and decisiveness of Lt Gen. Sagat Singh

SOME people are born to lead, but even these born warrior leaders must learn professionalism in modern warfare before they can successfully lead men in battle. Sagat was one such man. He joined the Bikaner State Forces as a Naik, and within a short time, was promoted as an officer in Sardul Light Infantry (now 19 Rajput) just before it moved to Iraq during World War II. By the time the unit returned to India, after four years, he had been nominated to attend the Staff College at Quetta. What qualities made this man, who was more comfortable speaking in the vernacular, achieve these heights?

Dhaka had been surrounded in one of the swiftest and greatest feats of arms in less than sixteen days. Lt Gen. Sagat's vision, which he kept close to his chest, saw him use all the resources at his disposal innovatively. Sagat had this constant yearning to learn and to achieve. He always volunteered for any professional course allotted to the battalion. Such was his ability that he was made to do the Staff Course at Haifa in 1943–44; he was maybe the only Indian officer to be nominated to do two staff courses. Sagat commanded two battalions of the 3rd Gorkha Rifles and was serving in Army HQ as a Colonel when the COAS picked him up in an unprecedented step to command the 50 Para Brigade. A normal infantry officer never got such an appointment. Sagat did his jumps quickly and got down to training his brigade when he was asked to move to Belgaum for the liberation of Goa in 1961.

The Para Brigade was allotted the subsidiary axis in the north from Sawantwadi, while the main body, consisting of 17 Infantry Division, moved from Belgaum, across the Sahyadris, from east to west, into Goa. Sagat had no bridging equipment but had four main rivers to cross in his advance. The Army Commander (later COAS), Lt Gen. JN Chaudhuri, had little expectation of the Para Brigade achieving anything much, but Sagat bet Brig. DK Palit, Director of Military Operations, that he would be in Panjim first. The stakes were a drink at the Mandovi Hotel bar.

On the face of it, Sagat had little chance of making it first, pitted against the resources of a whole division as he was. On top of that, he had only two Para battalions and was allotted an under-equipped and under-trained 2 Sikh LI only, at their concentration area in Belgaum. Sagat was a hard task master and did his best to get the battalion into shape.

The advance commenced on 18 December. The Para
Brigade would move directly south and link up with 17
Infantry Division at Pillem, while 2 Sikh LI, with an armoured
squadron, was to move on a parallel axis to Mapuca, which was
opposite Panjim and separated by the Mandovi river. It was the
intention of the division commander to enter the Portuguese
capital with his division. Sagat had this great quality of not
breathing down his subordinates' necks, and he allowed the
Para battalions to use their own heads while he spent time with
2 Sikh LI, encouraging them to accelerate their advance. The
Paras crossed three rivers by ad hoc means and kept advancing
till nightfall when Sagat called a halt as 17 Infantry Division
had still not linked up. By then, straining at the leash, 1 Para
had captured Ponda, an objective of the division, and 2 Para
was on the road to Panjim.

50 Para Brigade had ringed the capital from three directions.
17 Infantry Division was still out of communication when the
Army Commander decided that night to allow 50 Para Brigade
to recommence its advance. That was enough. The 2 Sikh
LI, emboldened as never before, crossed the Mandovi in the
morning and entered Panjim, while 1 Para made a dash and
captured the seat of government. Brig. Palit flew down to Goa
and paid for the drink with Sagat.

Sagat's grand achievement catapulted him as the cynosure of
all eyes in the army. He had this unique ability of understanding
a situation more rapidly than anyone else and then acting on
it decisively. For him, the fog of war dispersed more rapidly.
He would remain cool and calculating despite the fluidity of
the battle. He was anything but orthodox, and imbued his
command with his confidence, daring and courage, and allowed
them their initiative, too.

After his National Defence College (NDC) Course, Sagat was posted as Brigadier General Staff at HQ 11 Corps. Just before the 1965 Indo-Pak war, he was posted as Division Commander of 17 Mountain Division, deployed on the Sikkim Watershed. In those days, troops deployed on the Watershed acted as a trip wire against any Chinese ingress and carried out delay and warning up to the main defences, which were in depth. Sagat realized that giving up the Watershed would entail a most difficult operation in the re-occupation of it. It would also enable the enemy to roll down more easily towards Gangtok. He gave orders that the Watershed would not be given up and set about shoring up its defences. He was soon put to the test as the Chinese started pushing the defences in solidarity with Pakistan. Sagat's orders were firm. Troops will hold on, regardless. The neighbouring formation, as per orders, gave up Jelep La and deployed main defences in the depth. Since then, the Chinese have held Jelep La and India has not been able to recover it. Despite instructions, Sagat denied the enemy the Watershed and that is why we continue to hold Nathu La and Cho La.

Bent on preventing the continuous Chinese pinpricks at Nathu La, Sagat decided to lay a fence on the Watershed. He took his superiors on board and a single strand of barbed wire was laid on 18 August 1967, despite physical interference and intimidation by the Chinese. The fence was being turned into a formidable obstacle. On 11 September, as work commenced, without warning the Chinese opened devastating small arms fire. There were heavy casualties and Sagat asked for permission to open artillery fire. As it was not forthcoming, he gave the orders nevertheless. Our domination of the Watershed enabled the observation posts to look deep into

Chinese territory. Heavy casualties resulted, and it took some time for the Chinese to recover.

Shortly after the situation stabilized, Sagat was posted as General Officer Commanding, 101 Area, with the responsibility to counter the insurgency in Mizoram. Counter-insurgency operations multiplied, with small teams to the fore. Junior officers were allowed to exercise initiative and take responsibility for operations. Sagat carried out a parallel initiative in the resettlement of villages as well as in winning the hearts and minds of the people there. By the time he got posted out, Sagat had ensured that the back of insurgency had been broken.

Sagat was posted as General Officer Commanding, 4 Corps, in December 1970, and was awarded a Param Vishisht Seva Medal (PVSM) on 26 January. Meanwhile, East Pakistan was in turmoil. There was no alternative but to exercise the military option. On account of climate and terrain constraints, this could only be done in December. Sagat got to know of the role he was to play in July 1971. Operational instructions were issued in August. He moved to Tripura in September. He was allocated the counter-insurgency formations of 8 and 57 Mountain Divisions and was also allotted his reserve, 23 Mountain Division. Several ad hoc forces were created, prominent among them being the K Force, which was to play a major role in the advance to Chittagong. To create administrative maintenance areas in a short time for such a large force under the most hostile circumstances was a major achievement.

The initial task required 4 Corps to advance up to the Meghna river line, capture Chittagong, if possible, and contain Sylhet. Sagat was not satisfied with his tasking. Dhaka was the lynchpin of the Theatre Offensive, but it was not mentioned anywhere as an objective. Sagat had little time to train his units in conventional operations, but carefully monitored their activities. Before the offensive, there were three brigade-level operations. Not satisfied with some of the performances, Sagat was brutal in telling his commanders and troops that he would not accept foot-dragging.

The Corps offensive started by the end of November, which required the initial crust of the enemy defences to be pierced. The most savage fighting was opposite Agartala, where 57 Mountain Division was tasked to capture Akhaura. It was a slogging match lasting five days, and Sagat set the tone by venturing ahead of the forward troops in a helicopter and then landing among them to encourage them on. He allowed no rest as the enemy front started crumbling.

The habit he established initially set the tone of the campaign. His formations were spread over a large geographical area. The Northern Sector was where the offensive was being carried out by 8 Mountain Division towards Sylhet. The North-Central Sector was with 57 Mountain Division as it advanced from Agartala. The South-Central Sector was under 23 Mountain Division as it advanced towards the river port of Chandpur, and the Southern Sector was under the ad hoc K Force, which was tasked to head south towards Chittagong.

Every day Sagat would range over his entire frontage in an Allouette helicopter of the Air Force (subsequently, he started using an Air OP flight helicopter piloted by Major, later Lt Gen., GS Sihota). He would take flight at the crack of dawn, mostly as per an itinerary chalked out late the previous night. He would visit the formations, sometimes flying ahead of the forward troops and landing among them, constantly encouraging them while giving them critical information about the enemy. There were times when he would change focus, seeing the progress of the offensive. He would land back at the Corps HQ, sometimes after last light, and then, after a quick wash, would head for the Operations Room. Thereafter, he and the senior staff would go to the A Mess, where he would issue orders for the next day, sending his staff into a tizzy. At times the plans would change completely. For Sagat, written instructions were only pieces of paper.

The first major change occurred when he allowed 23 Mountain Division to infiltrate between the enemy defences rather than hit them head-on. The second was when the first heli-borne operation of the Indian Army was carried out on a shoestring. After reconnaissance by Group Captain Chandan Singh, on the night of 7 December, 4/5 GR, with a company of 9 Guards, was landed near the Surma bridges at Sylhet. The Mi-4 was an old war horse and had seen its best days, but along with the pilots, it performed marvellously. Instead of contesting the landing, the Pakistani units hemmed themselves in, waiting to be overwhelmed.

The previous day, 6 December, was also the day when Sagat carried out drastic changes to his plan. 57 Mountain Division, which had been tasked to head for the Meghna on an axis north of Maynamati, was ordered to continue its advance ahead of Akhaura towards Brahmanbaria. Taking 61 Brigade under his command, Sagat ordered it to head for Daudkandi on the Meghna while shedding two battalions to contain and attack the enemy defences on Lalmai Heights. The 8 Mountain Division was asked to get a brigade ready for a heli-borne operation on Dhaka. Sagat was a battle opportunist par excellence.

Suspecting what Sagat had in mind, the Army Commander rang him on 7 December and told him firmly not to attempt a crossing of the Meghna. This led to an acrimonious argument between them, resulting in Aurora visiting Sagat on 8 December. Sagat managed to convince him to allow him to go ahead with his plans.

The 9th of December was an extraordinary day, even for Sagat. He flew to Daudkandi on the Meghna and found it to be vacated. Then he flew south along the river to Chandpur, where he found no enemy, so he flew rearwards, landed in front of the leading battalion and the armoured squadron, picked up their commanding officers, showed them Chandpur from the air and dropped them back, telling them to go hell for leather. He flew to Daudkandi and landed in front of the leading company commander and told him to rush for the river and commandeer all the boats. Thereafter he flew to Agartala and picked up the Air Force squadron commanders to fly along the Meghna to do a recce of likely landing sites. While returning, he saw explosions near the only bridge at Ashuganj and flew over it. A machine gun opened fire, injuring the pilot and grazing the General. He returned to Agartala, had the pilot evacuated, commandeered another helicopter and flew to Brahmanbaria, where he saw the preparations for the famous 'Meghna Air Bridge' going on. He met Lt Col (later Lt Gen.) Himmeth Singh, Commanding Officer (CO) of 4 Guards, and others involved in the heli-borne operation being planned over the Meghna and returned to the Corps HQ late in the evening, where he allowed his injury to be treated.

The 4 Guards with other troops was flown over the Meghna at night. Other units took river crafts across. The squadron of

63 Cavalry, under Maj. Shamsher Mehta, which was right in the forefront of the advance, swam across. By the time Dhaka surrendered, it had been encircled from three sides—from the East across Daudkandi, and from the north-east and north. Indian brigades had successfully crossed the Meghna and carried on advancing, while the Pakistan brigade in opposition, with the GOC of their 14 Division, was successfully contained at Bhairab Bazaar.

Dhaka, as has been mentioned earlier, had been surrounded in one of the swiftest and greatest feats of arms in less than sixteen days. Sagat's vision, which he kept closely guarded, used resources optimally and innovatively; he did not give up on his aim and relentlessly pursued, bypassed and defeated the enemy. He was ruthless in the pursuit of this vision but ensured that his troops and commanders were imbued with enthusiasm for it. His personal courage, stamina and far-sightedness have never been matched in the annals of the Indian Army, which covered itself in glory on his account.

The Triumphant Race to Dhaka

Ajay Banerjee

In July 1971, the future capital of Bangladesh was not the final military objective. India looked to block and isolate East Pakistan, preventing withdrawal to the western sector or the arrival of reinforcements of the enemy forces. The original plan of 4 Corps was to advance up to Meghna river; it was quick thinking by India to cross it for a decisive push

'I give you thirty minutes to reconsider the decision not to surrender,' was the simple but stern message that Maj. Gen. (later Lt Gen.) JFR Jacob had for his Pakistani counterpart Lt Gen. AAK Niazi at about 11 a.m. on 16 December 1971. 'Hostilities and bombing Dacca (now Dhaka) would resume,' the rotund, pipe-smoking, but otherwise soft-spoken general would add, leaving nothing to the imagination.

Lt Gen. Niazi and Pakistan were hoping for international intervention. A UN-mandated ceasefire was ordered. Maj. Gen. Jacob, backed by the spectacular encircling of Dacca by the Indian Army, got Lt Gen. Niazi to surrender at 4.30 p.m. on the same day; 93,000 troops were taken prisoners of war in East Pakistan.

In his autobiography, Lt Gen. Jacob recounts the meeting: 'As I made this offer, I was worried. Pakistan had some 26,000 troops in Dacca, we had about 3,000 and those too some 30 miles out.'

The 'race to Dacca' has enjoyed relatively less focus as against the battles in the western sector during the 1971 war. It was immaculate planning, decisive thrusts and calculated risk-taking that led to the abject surrender of the Pakistan military and the birth of a new nation.

Between 3 and 16 December, troops under the 2 Corps, 33 Corps and 4 Corps approached Dacca from multiple directions, and some pitched battles were fought all along. On the western border of East Pakistan (facing West Bengal), the newly raised 2 Corps and 33 Corps made a push, beating the Pakistan army comprehensively.

A week of spectacular events

The decisive thrust came from the 4 Corps, which was on the eastern flank of East Pakistan and approached it from Assam, Tripura and Mizoram to finally reach Dacca. This was in an era without live satellite imagery or the tactical reconnaissance capability of drones. The outcome of battles

was largely dependent on the resilience of a ground attack—
by infantry, tanks, artillery and para-forces. All these attacks
had to be backed by ground intelligence, military engineers,
communications and the ingenious use of equipment.
However, the final push towards Dacca from 9 December is an
enthralling run of events.

Dacca is wedged between two mighty rivers—the
Padma/Brahmaputra to its west and the Meghna to its east.
The 4 Corps reached the eastern bank of the Meghna on 9
December, twelve days ahead of plan. They began the task of
first crossing to the west bank, as Pakistan had blown up the
bridge at Bhairab Bazaar, about 80 kms from Dacca. Six days
later, Indian troops, tanks and artillery encircled Dacca just in
time for Jacob to famously give 'thirty minutes' to Niazi. The
USSR used its veto power at the UNSC from 3 to 14 December
to hold back international pressure, and the ceasefire was
announced on 15 December. But before this, crucial battles
were fought. Notably, the 4th battalion of 5 Gorkha Rifles,
despite casualties, stuck to a tactical position in Sylhet to hold
back two brigades of the Pakistan army.

Niazi's plan scuttled

Lt Gen. Niazi, the governor of East Pakistan and commander
of the Eastern Command, had used some seven brigades
(of around 5,000 men each), besides paramilitary, to forge
a 'fortress policy'. This included turning a number of major
towns into defensive positions. The Indian Army used all
elements, from tanks to artillery, and from paratroopers to
infantry to helicopters, to counter these positions, while also
finding alternative routes to move ahead.

The Pakistani plan was to stall the Indian advance at these 'fortresses' and after a point fall back to Dacca, making it 'impregnable' and holding it till international intervention would ask India to back off. Pakistani defences held large obstacles: water courses and deep rivers. The Indian Army avoided these, and here came out-of-the-box thinking, such as the use of tanks in the riverine terrain and heli-lift of a brigade across the Meghna.

The final thrust

Around the evening of 9 December, the 4 Corps started its famous crossing of the Meghna river. Within five days it had lined up nine infantry battalions and, supported by artillery, tanks and engineers, it was ready to assault Dacca. Jacob arrived at 11 a.m. for the meeting with Lt Gen. Niazi. This was followed by a public surrender ceremony, but hours before that, Indian troops had reached the outskirts of Dacca. The 2 Para, under Brig. Sant Singh, and a part of the 101 Communication Zone, led by Maj. Gen. G Nagra, had got Mirpur bridge (located on the outskirts of Dacca) vacated. The 8 Mountain Division came down from Sylhet and closed in on Dacca. The first tanks of the 5 Independent Squadron of 63 Cavalry rolled into Dacca.

In July 1971, India's military plans did not talk about Dacca being the final objective. India looked to block and isolate East Pakistan, segmenting Pakistani defences to prevent their withdrawal or entry of reinforcements. The original plan of the 4 Corps was to advance to only up to the Meghna. It was quick thinking to first cross it and then race towards Dacca.

Trident and Python, the Defining Operations

Cmde Srikant Kesnur and Lt Cdr Divyajot

A recap of the devastating attacks on Karachi on 4 and 8 December

THE Indo-Pak war of 1971 for the liberation of Bangladesh was IN's finest hour. The Navy fought in two separate theatres and established total control in both the Arabian Sea and the Bay of Bengal. Its ships and aircraft sank enemy ships, destroyed shore infrastructure and completely dominated the PN. Many units and personnel of the IN covered themselves with glory. However, arguably, the events that most captured the public imagination were the devastating attacks on Karachi on 4 and 8 December. A recap of the operation, five decades later, attempts to highlight its salient aspects.

But, first, a brief background. In the 1965 war, the Indian Navy was assigned a defensive role and was directed not to operate north of Porbandar. This was to result, among other things, in a furtive raid on Dwarka by the Pakistan Navy. While it was completely inconsequential and resulted in no damage, it led to some uninformed criticism of the Indian Navy. It also caused a lot of disquiet in the rank and file about being deprived of action and about the Navy's inherent flexibility not being utilized. The Navy's senior officers were determined that should another opportunity arise, the Service must not be 'found wanting', and this opportunity presented itself six years later. In the intervening period, the Navy's leadership had also rapidly increased its manpower and augmented its hardware by acquiring submarines, Petya-class corvettes and Osa-class missile boats, all of which played an important role in the war.

As soon as hostilities commenced, with Pakistan declaring a full-fledged war on 3 December, the orders for Op. Trident were dispatched to the fleet at Mumbai and Okha. Op. Trident comprised three missile boats (IN ships *Nirghat*, *Nipat* and *Veer*) and two Petya-class ships (*Katchal* and *Kiltan*), which were to accompany the missile boats, unleash them at dark close to Karachi at full speed and carry out missile attacks. They would also maintain a lookout with their superior sensor capabilities. *Nipat* and *Veer* sailed out from Mumbai and *Nirghat* from Okha. They met mid-sea off Diu and sailed together from there for the attack.

This daring raid resulted in the sinking of *PNS Khaibar*, *PNS Muhafiz* and *MV Venus Challenger*, and the setting of fire on the Kemari oil refinery.

The Navy sustained the momentum by following up with Op. Python on 8 December, which caused further destruction of Pakistani assets. In this operation, involving missile attacks by *INS Vinash*, supported by *INS Trishul* and *INS Talwar*, *PNS Dacca* and *MV Harmattan* were severely damaged, *MV Gulf Star* destroyed and the Kemari oil field set ablaze again. The magnitude of devastation was so large and unexpected that PN withdrew ships inside the Karachi harbour and ordered de-ammunition. Thus, the maritime war on the western front was effectively over within five days of commencement of hostilities.

The success of Op. Trident is celebrated as Navy Day each year. It was acknowledged as a great military feat by many, including Adm. Gorshkov of the Soviet Navy as the Russians themselves had never envisaged this role for the missile boats.

Meticulous planning at various echelons, months of exercises and trials to hone skills, as well as spirited execution by the missile boat squadron went a long way in ensuring the success of the operation. It is also necessary to acknowledge the strong political backing which this audacious plan received.

Many aspects of the attacks were novel—the use of missiles in this region for the first time, the resort to towing of smaller vessels by bigger ships to overcome the problem of endurance, radio silence and ingenious methods of communication to remain undetected, and the use of vessels meant for coastal defence in an offensive role.

The celebration of the Killer Squadron's feat would be incomplete if it does not include the role of the men involved in the naval planning and acquisition, especially Adm. AK Chatterji (after whose initials the vessels are named) and his staff, who were prescient in acquiring these small missile boats from the Soviet Union. However, above all, the 'bombing of Karachi' is owed to one man who combined conviction, offensive spirit and risk-taking ability—Adm. SM (Charles) Nanda, the Navy Chief during the war. It was his strategy of destroying the war-fighting capability of the enemy that played an important role in determining the outcome of the war.

The exploits of the Indian Navy and the 25th Missile Boat Squadron, more popularly known as the Killer Squadron, are ingrained in the collective memory. Op. Trident and Op. Python carried the attack into the very citadel of the enemy. With these attacks, the young Indian Navy had earned its spurs and come of age.

At the PoW Camp with Khaliq, Who Lost to Milkha

Lt Col AK Ahlawat

Recalling the chance meeting of Col Krishan Lal Wahi with the legendary Pakistani athlete, his request for medical aid for a fellow soldier and how the Colonel's son offered to donate blood to a Pakistani soldier

IT was 20 December 1971, and the war had ended a few days ago. Ajay was a pre-medical student in DAV College, Chandigarh. He reached the Chandigarh bus stand to catch the first bus to Jammu. The morning was cool and a winter's haze hung on the roofs of the lined-up buses. A few minutes before 7 a.m., the Sikh driver in khaki climbed behind the wheel of the bus. By evening, Ajay was with his father, Col Krishan Lal

Wahi, posted at Udhampur, where the Army's 15 Corps was headquartered. The family was grieving. On 6 December, they had lost Flight Lieutenant Vijay Kumar Wahi in aerial battles over Chhamb–Akhnoor. He was flying a Sukhoi 7 with the IAF's 101 Fighter Squadron. The mood at home was sombre and quiet. Vijay Wahi was the hero brother, the fighter pilot brother whom Ajay hero-worshipped.

Then one day his father said, 'Ajay, I have to visit the Prisoner of War camp here in Udhampur. Would you like to come along?'

So they drove out in an Army Jonga, turned left from the nullah before the Base Hospital and reached the barbed wire cage of the PoW camp. The time-scale Colonel, an elderly Sikh who was the camp commandant, took them to his hut and gave them tea and biscuits.

'Anyone from Khooshab Sargodha area in the camp?' asked Colonel Wahi.

'I think there might be a few,' he said, pressing the office bell. An orderly appeared.

'Go call the Pakistani senior JCO.'

A man in khaki came in, saluted and disclosed his name, number, rank and unit.

'JCOs are at gun position in the rear. How did you get caught as PoW?' asked Col Wahi.

'Janab, there is a lot of difference in our armies. In the Indian Army, officers do Artillery Observation Post duty. In our army, officers remain behind at gun positions and JCOs are at Forward Observation Posts to direct artillery fire. My observation post got over-run by the Indian infantry and I was taken prisoner.'

Col Wahi was silent for a few moments, trying to recollect something. 'Isn't there a Pakistani athlete of your name who had competed against Milkha Singh in races?' he asked.

The Pakistani came to stiff attention and said, 'Janab, I am the same man.'

Subedar Abdul Khaliq of 8 Medium Regiment was an ace sprinter whom Pandit Nehru had called the 'The Flying Bird of Asia'. When Milkha Singh won against him, Pakistan President Gen. Ayub Khan had called the legendary Indian athlete, who passed away from post-Covid complications in June 2021 at the age of 91, the 'Flying Sikh'.

Col Wahi and Subedar Khaliq exchanged notes about their native province for some time, and then the JCO asked, '*Gustakhi mauf howey tan janab ek arz karan* (Sir, if you permit, I have an appeal).'

'*Bilkul dasso* (Sure, go ahead).'

'*Janab eik munda hai, ohh nu bayonet lagya hai. Doctor saab roz aande ne, oh nuu dekhdey ney, parr ohh thik nahi ho rayaa* (Sir, there is a soldier of ours who has a bayonet wound, the doctor comes every day to attend to him but his condition is not improving).'

'*Badaa tezz bukhaar hai mundey nuu aur saadey paasey daa he hai* (The lad has high fever and he is from our province).'

He asked if a surgeon could have a look at him as he was slipping away fast and maybe his life could be saved.

The senior surgery adviser at the Base Hospital was a white-bearded Sikh who too hailed from Khooshab. He was Col Wahi's tennis partner. They gave him a call and explained the case to him. The surgeon, Colonel Baldev Singh, asked for the PoW to be sent to the Base Hospital and sent an ambulance.

In the evening, the surgeon met Col Wahi at the tennis court. The young schoolboy also accompanied his father.

'Thank God you sent him just in time. The bayonet has gone deep inside and he has peritonitis. Very serious infection has developed inside and he will have to be operated upon. We need some blood for him. I have told the staff that I will operate after I play tennis and in the meantime, they are to look for some donor of the same blood group.'

Ajay Wahi, who was overhearing the conversation, asked, 'Sir, what blood group is he?'

'He is B Positive.'

'I am also B Positive.'

The surgeon looked at Ajay, 'You will donate blood to this Pakistani soldier?'

'Yes, I will.'

'Are you sure?'

'Of course I will.'

'Come son, then let's go to the hospital.'

They reached the hospital and the senior surgeon said, 'Here is the voluntary donor, I will just change and operate.'

Then the father and son came back. The father said, 'Son, I thought that you were still a kid, but I have realized today that my son is no longer a boy, he is a man.'

Lt Col Ajay Wahi, a pathologist, donated blood 130 times till he reached the age of sixty-five.

An All-Too-Familiar Face Among Pak PoWs

Wg Cdr JS Bhalla (Retd)

Recalling the surreal encounter at Kolkata two months after the 1971 war

CAPT. Karamjit Singh Sodhi, a retired merchant navy officer, was a junior navigating officer in 1971 when he joined *MV Andaman*, a passenger ship of the Shipping Corporation. In February 1972, when *MV Andaman* was berthed in Kolkata, they were asked to prepare themselves for embarking the next morning on an important mission. As the ship sailed out, they were told that they were on a mission to bring back Pakistani prisoners of war (PoWs) from Bangladesh to Kolkata.

The war had ended two months back, but fear was writ large on many faces on the ship because it was known that the Pakistanis had mined the approach to the Chittagong harbour. The vessel arrived at Chittagong safely, and with the help of the local pilot it sailed up to Karnaphuli river, which was strewn with the remnants of bombarded and sunk merchant ships—a testament to the brave actions of the IAF and pilots of *INS Vikrant*.

In the evening, Sodhi went out for a meal and saw the local population raising slogans of '*Indian-Bangla Bhai Bhai*'.

No rickshaw-wallah or restaurant owner would accept any money from him. It was the valour displayed by the Indian armed forces that generated respect in the hearts of the local population, he realized.

The following day, 1,500 PoWs, escorted by the Indian Army, were brought to the ship. Officers up to the rank of Major were assigned the space meant for lady passengers in the ship. The senior officers were kept in the ship hospital, which could accommodate about ten of them. The PoWs cooked their own meals in the galley, while senior officers were brought to the officers' mess and were served the same food as the ship officers.

When the ship berthed at Kolkata's King George dock, an Indian Army Colonel took charge and went through the list of the PoWs. He wanted to meet the senior-most officer, who was of the rank of Commodore. Sodhi was detailed to bring the Commodore from the ship hospital.

When the Colonel saw the Commodore, both of them saluted and addressed each other as 'Sir'. They shook hands. Their eyes were moist but neither uttered a word; however, their body language indicated that they knew each other.

Later, it was revealed that before Independence, the Colonel was a cadet in the same training institute where the Commodore had been an instructor. At the time of Partition, the two had gone on separate paths but *MV Andaman* had brought them face to face once again, though this time their loyalties, like the circumstances, were all too different.

Lest We Forget, the Veer Naris of the 1971 War

Maj. Ishleen Kaur

The women who sacrificed for the country

THE history of any army is replete with immortalized tales of selflessness, camaraderie and the ultimate sacrifice. While soldiers who have brought victory have been inscribed in the memories of the country as 'Forever Young', there are women who have faced the brunt of these wars—not by facing the nameless bullet, but by bravely living the turbulent life that comes after a war. On the fiftieth anniversary of the 1971 Indo-Pak War, and to commemorate the victory, homage is being paid to the fallen, and respects to the veterans and Veer Naris along the length and breadth of the country.

As the Akhnoor-based Crossed Swords Division commenced on a humble odyssey to pay respects to its veterans and felicitate its Veer Naris, what emerged were stories of courage, valour, hardship and sacrifice. The Division set out to recognize and felicitate the wives, mothers and daughters of the men who returned home wrapped in the Tricolour without a chance to say their words of farewell to their loved ones.

'I do not want to be called a victim of war. I was strong enough to survive on my own,' a Veer Nari famously said, echoing the sentiments of many like her. To understand the story of a soldier, one must fathom the depth of emotion in their moist eyes. The war left us with many such stories, but those of Git Kaur, Kanta Devi, Karnataro Devi, Simro Devi and Pushpa Devi can melt any heart. These women were at the height of marital bliss, proud to be married to men who donned the olive green in a society that has a rich martial tradition, when their husbands passed away. Belonging to Jammu and nearby areas, these Veer Naris have struggled to live their lives without their husbands for the past fifty years, but have emerged as stellar examples of what true grit, determination and courage mean.

Git Kaur, wife of the late Sepoy Balwant Singh of the 5th Battalion, Sikh Regiment, lives a mere 30 km from Chhamb–Jaurian, the place where her husband made the supreme sacrifice. A mother of two, the younger of whom never saw her father, she recounts how the indomitable spirit she imbibed from her husband pushed her on when times seemed bleak, with the relentless support of the Army.

Kanta Devi, wife of the late Havildar Amarnath, Sena Medal, of the 8th Battalion of JAK Light Infantry, still vividly remembers her husband's playful jokes. He would tell her that

the Army would be with her long after he had gone. He lost
his life defending his homeland just 15 km from his home in
Sunderbani. The times that followed were tough; goons and
thugs, assuming that she would be a soft target, tried to extort
money from her, but were warded off with the assistance of the
Army. Her two sons and a daughter, one of whom serves in the
Central Reserve Police Force (CRPF), are now well settled and
happily married.

Karnataro Devi, wife of the late Sepoy Sundurilal of the
5th Battalion of the Dogra Regiment, came to know about her
husband's martyrdom three months after the war when his
mortal remains arrived, as the roads from Kargil were blocked
due to the hazardous weather. But fate had yet more tests for
her; she lost her young son to an ailment soon after. However,
with a will to fight on, she rallied her courage and worked
even harder to provide the best for her daughter, the last living
symbol of her eternal bond with a brave soldier.

The story of Simro Devi, wife of the late Sepoy Sahib Singh
of the 9th Battalion of JAK Light Infantry, is yet another tale
to draw inspiration from. Only a mirage remained of the
dreams the couple had woven together, of having a daughter
and bringing her up with love and care. After the demise of
her husband, life changed for Simro Devi, and gloom lay heavy
upon the young woman. Nevertheless, she found her inner
strength and took up tailoring to lead a life of respect and
dignity. She adopted a girl and, honouring the wishes of her
late husband, raised her the way they had dreamt of.

The moist eyes of Pushpa Devi, wife of the late Lance Naik
Gullu Ram of 8 Grenadiers, tell a story of perseverance without
a single word being uttered. Sorrow and grief may have wrinkled
her features, but not her spirit. Gullu Ram made the supreme

sacrifice while fighting the enemy in the battle of Chakra in the Shakargarh bulge.

These stories form a part of the tapestry that is the Indian Army and the countless sacrifices it has made for the country. They serve as an inspiration in these trying times of the Covid-19 pandemic, when uncertainty looms large. It sends out the message that even after such an ordeal, if a person can survive and thrive in this world, there is no obstacle that human endeavour cannot surmount.

The Param Vir Chakra
Awardees

Army

1. Major (later Colonel) Hoshiar Singh
2. Second Lieutenant Arun Khetarpal (Posthumous)
3. Lance Naik Albert Ekka (Posthumous)

Air Force

4. Flying Officer Nirmaljit Singh Sekhon (Posthumous)

Maj. Hoshiar Singh

COMMISSIONED into the 3rd Battalion of Grenadiers in 1963, Col Hoshiar Singh retired in 1988 after a splendid and inspiring military career, one that saw him earning the country's highest gallantry award, the Param Vir Chakra, as a Major during the 1971 war with Pakistan in the western sector. Enrolled as a Sepoy in the 2nd Jat Battalion (Mooltan), the 1936-born native of Sisana village (then in Rohtak and now in Haryana's Sonepat district) was eventually selected for the Army Cadet College.

Jarpal Complex and the surrounding areas in the Shakargarh sector were of strategic importance, and any continued dominance of the enemy here was considered a threat to the Pathankot–Jammu road, a vital link. The task of capturing Jarpal across Basantar nullah was given to 3 Grenadiers—

raised in 1768 as the 1st Sepoy Battalion, it has an impressive tally of gallantry awards.

In the Battle of Basantar, the iconic battle to capture and hold Jarpal, it was Major Hoshiar Singh who was in command of Charlie Company of 3 Grenadiers. The citation for the PVC awarded to him reads:

On December 15, 1971, 3 Grenadiers was given the task of establishing a bridgehead across Basantar river in Shakargarh sector. For accomplishment of the mission, the enemy locality named Jarpal had to be captured first. Major Hoshiar Singh, who was commanding the left forward company, was ordered to attack and capture Jarpal, which was well fortified and held in strength by the enemy. During the assault, his company came under intense artillery shelling and effective crossfire from the enemy medium machine guns. Undeterred, Major Hoshiar Singh led the charge and captured the objective after a fierce hand-to-hand fight.

The enemy reacted sharply and put in three successive counter-attacks supported by armour on December 16. Major Hoshiar Singh, unmindful of heavy shelling and tank fire, went from trench to trench motivating his men and encouraging them to remain steadfast and fight. Inspired by his dauntless leadership, his company repulsed all counter-attacks, inflicting heavy casualties on the enemy. Again, on December 17, the enemy launched another massive counter-attack with a battalion supported by medium artillery fire. Though seriously wounded, Major Hoshiar Singh, with total disregard to personal safety, continued to inspire his men by going from platoon to platoon even under intense artillery shelling.

When an enemy artillery shell landed near the machine gun post seriously injuring the crew and rendering the machine gun inoperative, Major Hoshiar Singh, realising the importance of machine gun fire, immediately rushed to the machine gun pit and though seriously wounded, manned the gun, inflicting heavy casualties onto the enemy. The counter-attack was repulsed yet again and the enemy retreated, leaving behind 85 dead, including Lieutenant Colonel Akram Raja, their commanding officer, and three other officers. Major Hoshiar Singh, though seriously wounded, remained with his Charlie Company and refused to be evacuated till the ceasefire.

Throughout the operation, Major Hoshiar Singh displayed most conspicuous gallantry, indomitable fighting spirit and unparalleled leadership.

A keen volleyball player, Major Hoshiar Singh, PVC, also did a stint at the IMA after the war as Company Commander and as Colonel commanded his own battalion, 3 Grenadiers, also known as the PVC battalion.

Col Hoshiar Singh, PVC, passed away on 6 December 1998. Two of his three sons followed in his footsteps and were commissioned into Grenadiers.

The Tribune

Second Lt Arun Khetarpal
(Posthumous)

A Param Vir at twenty-one, Second Lt Arun Khetarpal from
The Poona Horse continues to capture the imagination
of every Indian and has rightfully attained legendary status.
A fourth-generation soldier, Arun studied at Lawrence
School, Sanawar, before being selected for the NDA. He was
commissioned into The Poona Horse—among the highest
decorated cavalry regiments, with a combination of a squadron
each of Jats, Sikhs and Rajputs—on 13 June 1971.

Tank battles raged in the western theatre in December at
Barapind and Jarpal in the Basantar Nadi area of Pakistan's
Zafarwal–Shakargarh sector. Many fierce encounters took
place between the tanks of 16 Independent Armoured Brigade,
comprising The Poona Horse and Hodson's Horse (16 Cavalry,

the third regiment, was deployed in a defensive posture), and of 13 Lancers and 31 Cavalry of the Pakistan army's 8 Independent Armoured Brigade.

Around 9 a.m. on 16 December, the tanks of Capt. V Malhotra, Lieutenant Avtar Ahlawat and 2/Lt Arun Khetarpal were involved in the iconic battle at Jarpal.

Lt Ahlawat's tank was hit, Capt Malhotra's developed a snag, and for nearly half an hour it was all left to Lt Arun Khetarpal to hold the fort. He knocked off four Patton tanks, and when his own tank, 'Famagusta', was hit and caught fire, he refused to abandon it as the gun was still firing. The lone fighter died when his tank received another direct hit.

Second Lt Arun Khetarpal was posthumously awarded the Param Vir Chakra. His citation reads:

> On December 16, 1971, the Squadron Commander of 'B' Squadron, The Poona Horse, asked for reinforcements as the Pakistani armour, which was superior in strength, counter-attacked Jarpal in the Shakargarh sector. On hearing this transmission on the regimental net, Second Lieutenant Arun Khetarpal, who was in 'A' Squadron, voluntarily moved along with his troop to assist the other Squadron. En route, while crossing the Basantar river, Second Lieutenant Arun Khetarpal and his troop came under fire from enemy strong points and RCL gun nests that were still holding out. Time was at a premium and as a critical situation was developing in 'B' Squadron sector, Second Lieutenant Arun Khetarpal threw caution to the winds and started attacking the impending enemy strong points by literally charging them, overrunning the defence works with his tanks

and capturing the enemy infantry and weapon crews at pistol-point. In the course of one such daring attack, one tank commander of his troop was killed. Khetarpal continued to attack relentlessly until all enemy opposition was overcome and he broke through towards 'B' Squadron position, just in time to see the enemy tanks pulling back after their initial probing attack.

He was so carried away by wild enthusiasm of battle and the impetus of his own headlong dash that he started chasing the withdrawing tanks and even managed to shoot and destroy one. Soon thereafter, the enemy reformed with a squadron of armour for a second attack and this time, they selected the sector held by Second Lieutenant Arun Khetarpal and two other tanks as the point for their main effort. A fierce tank fight ensued; 10 enemy tanks were hit and destroyed of which Second Lieutenant Arun Khetarpal personally destroyed four but in that fierce engagement, he himself was severely wounded. He was told to abandon his tank but he realised that the enemy, though badly decimated, was continuing to advance and if he abandoned his tank, the enemy would break through; he gallantly fought on and destroyed another enemy tank. At this stage, his tank received a second hit which resulted in the death of this gallant officer.

Second Lieutenant Arun Khetarpal was dead but he had, by his intrepid valour, saved the day; the enemy was denied the breakthrough which he was so desperately seeking. Not one enemy tank got through.

Second Lieutenant Arun Khetarpal had shown the best qualities of leadership, tenacity of purpose and the will to close in. His was an act of dauntless courage and self-sacrifice far beyond the call of duty.

Three decades after the war, Arun Khetarpal's father, Brig. ML Khetarpal, a decorated Sapper himself, met Brig. Khwaja Naser of the Pakistan army, the man who is believed to have fired the fatal shot at Arun's tank. On display was deep mutual respect for each other's militaries.

The Tribune

Lance Naik Albert Ekka
(Posthumous)

WHEN the PAF bombed Indian airfields at 4.30 p.m. on 3 December 1971, it marked the commencement of hostilities. But even before the declaration of war, the Indian Army had to its credit two decisive victories in East Pakistan.

The 14 Punjab (Nabha Akal), with direct support from 6 Field Regiment (artillery) and 'C' Squadron of 45 Cavalry (armour), won the first on the morning of 21 November at Garibpur, 7 km inside East Pakistan's western front. By 10.30 a.m. on 3 December, just hours before the war was declared, 14 Guards had destroyed the defences at Ganga Sagar complex inside the eastern front of East Pakistan, west of Agartala. And out of that battle emerged Lance Naik Albert Ekka, earning the first Param Vir Chakra during Operation 'Cactus Lily', commonly referred to as the Bangladesh war.

Born in the tribal village of Zari in Ranchi (now in Gumla district of Jharkhand) on 27 December 1942, Albert Ekka was an able marksman with bow and arrow, and an ace hockey player to boot. Subedar Maj. Bhagirath Soren of 7 Bihar spotted him while he was playing a match and got him enrolled in the battalion.

The 32 Guards was raised in 1968 and consisted of Ahirs from the Kumaon Regiment, Mazhabi Sikhs from the Sikh Light Infantry and Biharis from the Bihar Regiment, all in equal proportion. Rifleman Albert's 'C' Company of 7 Bihar was allotted to 32 Guards. In April 1971, the 32nd was re-designated as the 14th Battalion of the Brigade of Guards.

The Ganga Sagar complex inside East Pakistan comprised the railway station, Goal Gangail, Lilahat, Triangle and Mogra. It was during its capture that Lance Naik Albert Ekka of 14 Guards was awarded the Param Vir Chakra, posthumously. His citation reads:

At 2 am on December 3, 1971, Lance Naik Albert Ekka was part of the left forward Bravo Company of 14th Guards during the attack on the enemy defences at Ganga Sagar on the eastern front. It was a well-fortified position held in strength and in great depth by the enemy. The assaulting troops were subjected to intense artillery shelling and heavy small arms fire, but they charged the enemy on the objective and were soon locked in a bitter hand-to-hand combat. During that close-quarter battle, Lance Naik Albert Ekka noticed an enemy light machine gun inflicting heavy casualties on his company. With complete disregard to his personal safety, he charged towards the machine gun bunker, bayoneted the firing crew of two and silenced the machine gun. Though seriously wounded in this encounter, he continued to fight alongside his comrades through half-a-km deep objective, clearing bunker after bunker with undaunted courage.

Towards the northern end of the objective, one enemy medium machine gun opened up from the second storey of a well-fortified building, inflicting heavy casualties and holding up the attack. Once again, this gallant soldier, without giving a thought to his personal safety, despite his serious injuries and heavy volume of enemy fire, crawled forward till he reached the building and lobbed a grenade through the loophole of the bunker, killing one enemy and injuring the other. The medium machine gun, however, continued to fire. With outstanding courage and determination, Lance Naik Albert Ekka scaled a side wall and after boldly entering the bunker, bayoneted the enemy who was still firing. He silenced the machine gun, saving further casualties to his company and ensuring the success of the attack.

In this process, however, he received fatal injuries and succumbed to them after the capture of the objective.

In this action, Lance Naik Albert Ekka displayed the most conspicuous acts of valour and determination and made the supreme sacrifice in the best traditions of the Army.

The valour displayed by Lance Naik Albert Ekka continues to be an inspiration to the armed forces.

The Tribune

Flying Officer Nirmaljit Singh Sekhon (Posthumous)

SPRINTING out of an underground shelter as the tannoy (a term used to denote a public address system in older, colloquial British English) blares is bread-and-butter stuff for fighter pilots in the IAF as they respond to a scramble order to intercept intruding enemy aircraft. Not many, however, would have imagined in the wildest of their dreams that they would have to scramble their jets during an enemy bombing raid that involved four aircraft already in the process of dropping their bombs over targets on the airfield. This is exactly the situation that young Flying Officer Nirmaljit Singh Sekhon (26) found himself in on 14 December 1971 at the Srinagar airfield, as part of an air defence detachment of four Gnat fighters from 18 Squadron, also called the Flying Bullets.

Srinagar, during those days, was not a base that had a fighter squadron permanently located there on account of the restrictions imposed on India not to base fighter aircraft at air bases in J&K, following the UN-sponsored ceasefire in 1947–48. Strangely, this was not revised even after the 1965 India–Pakistan war. Air Marshal Manjit Singh Sekhon, himself a Vir Chakra awardee from the 1971 war for his exploits while flying Vampires from 121 Squadron out of Srinagar, and who was closely related to Nirmaljit Sekhon, recalls that the latter was full of 'josh'. Much older and hailing from Nirmaljit's village, Issewal in Ludhiana, he recalls having advised Nirmaljit to focus on becoming an officer in the IAF. He also remembers that both their squadrons were put up in the same officer's mess at Badami Bagh, and that during the conflict Nirmaljit would often walk up to his room and say in Punjabi, '*Dhuan udana hai*'—meaning he wanted to 'smoke out the Pakistanis in battle'.

Battle-inoculated well before his epic dogfight over Srinagar airfield, Nirmaljit Sekhon had escorted Manjit Sekhon's formation of Vampires a few days earlier as the latter attacked the Hajira Brigade of the Pakistan army and enemy artillery guns at Dwarandi, both in the Poonch sector. Unable to resist the temptation of joining the party, the Gnats emptied their guns on the targets after the Vampires completed their attack before returning to Srinagar.

Though Air Chief Marshal Lal had instituted several measures to improve early warning of incoming strike aircraft through a layered network of radars and MOPs, the mountainous terrain and valleys offered excellent cover for the enemy aircraft to conceal their approach while attacking airfields such as Srinagar. Therefore, the only way for air defence aircraft like the Gnats to intercept incoming strike aircraft was if they had at least five to six minutes' warning, which would allow them to scramble in two or three minutes. No such window was available on 14 December, the day that Nirmaljit Sekhon was part of a two-aircraft air defence mission that was on readiness at Srinagar.

Masking themselves with tactical finesse and penetrating the Srinagar valley with ease, a six-aircraft Sabre formation from the PAF's 26 Squadron, led by their squadron commander, Wing Commander Changezi, swooped down on the Srinagar airfield at 7.30 a.m. Comprising four aircraft for airfield attack and two staying high to provide air defence cover, the Sabres thought it would be a cakewalk for them and, like a few times earlier, they would exit the Valley before the Gnats were scrambled. This time, however, they did not expect the speed with which Flight Lieutenant BS Ghuman and Flying Officer Sekhon would scramble into the air. Having got airborne before Sekhon as the Number One, Ghuman gained height and turned around to pick up his Number Two, but lost sight of everything below as there was a thick layer of haze between 1,000 and 3,000 feet.

Sekhon, meanwhile, miraculously got airborne even as the first Sabre pair had dropped their bombs on the runway and the second pair was diving for the attack. So, you had two Sabres at over 750 km/hr, with Sekhon's Gnat behind one of them as he built up speed quickly and commenced manoeuvring to get a shot on the Sabre leader, while the other Sabre attempted to get behind him. Two Sabres dropped their load and headed home, while Changezi called on the two loitering Sabres to come into the fight from above. Despite being outnumbered 4:1, Sekhon fought on, calling for Ghuman to support him and forcing the Sabre behind him to exhaust its ammo. Unfortunately, Ghuman had lost contact in the haze and could not join the fray. Out of ammunition and vulnerable to the second pair of Sabres which had their ammo intact, Sekhon's aircraft was hit by several bursts of concentrated fire and went down close to Badgam, the site of another epic battle in November 1947, where Major Somnath Sharma was awarded a Param Vir Chakra as his company of 4 Kumaon stalled the enemy's advance towards the Srinagar airfield. Sekhon attempted an ejection, but was too close to the ground and perished in action. Among the Indian accounts of that battle, a 2017 piece by KS Nair in the *Indian Defence Review* and a terrific YouTube animation by Anurag Rana offer the finest accounts. Kaiser Tufail provides the best PAF perspective in his blog 'Aeronaut', where he calls Sekhon a 'hard nut to crack', and describes the combat with flair as Sekhon 'snatched degrees at a dizzying rate'.

While it is possible that Sekhon had scored a few hits and inflicted some damage on one of the Sabres, the PAF claims that all the Sabres returned to Peshawar undamaged. However, there is ungrudging admiration for Sekhon from all his adversaries who were involved in that day's combat. For his 'sublime heroism, supreme gallantry, flying skill and determination above and beyond the call of duty in the face of certain death', Flying Officer Nirmaljit Singh Sekhon was awarded the IAF's only Param Vir Chakra till date.

Air Vice Marshal
Arjun Subramaniam (Retd)

The Maha Vir Chakra
Awardees

Army

1. Brigadier Sant Singh, MVC and Bar
2. Brigadier (later General) Arun Sridhar Vaidya, MVC and Bar
3. Brigadier Kailash Prasad Pande
4. Lieutenant Colonel (later Major General) Kulwant Singh Pannu
5. Major (later Brigadier) Kuldip Singh Chandpuri
6. Brigadier (later Major General) Hardev Singh Kler
7. Brigadier (later Lieutenant General) Anand Sarup
8. Lieutenant Colonel (later Brigadier) Sawai Bhawani Singh
9. Lieutenant Colonel (later Brigadier) Sukhjit Singh
10. Major (later Brigadier) BS Mankotia
11. Lance Naik Shangara Singh (Posthumous)
12. Sepoy Anusuya Prasad (Posthumous)
13. Lieutenant Colonel (later Brigadier) Arun Bhimrao Harolikar
14. Rifleman (later Lance Havildar) Dil Bahadur Chhetri
15. Lieutenant Colonel (later Major General) Shamsher Singh
16. Second Lieutenant Shamsher Singh Samra (Posthumous)
17. Lance Naik Ram Ugrah Pandey (Posthumous)
18. Brigadier (later Lieutenant General) Joginder Singh Bakshi
19. Brigadier (later Major General) Antony Harold Edward Michigan
20. Lieutenant Colonel (later Major General) Chittoor Venugopal
21. Havildar (later Subedar Major) Bir Bahadur Pun

22. Major (later Brigadier) Vijay Kumar Berry
23. Major Vijay Rattan Chowdhary (Posthumous)
24. Captain Shankar Rao Walkar (Posthumous)
25. Captain Pradip Kumar Gour (Posthumous)
26. Brigadier (later Lieutenant General) Joginder Singh Gharaya
27. Lieutenant Colonel Surinder Kapur
28. Major Anup Singh Gahlaut (Posthumous)
29. Naik Sugan Singh (Posthumous)
30. Lieutenant Colonel Ved Prakash Ghai (Posthumous)
31. Lieutenant Colonel (later Lieutenant General) Ved Prakash Airy
32. Havildar (later Honorary Captain) Thomas Phillipose
33. Lieutenant Colonel (later Lieutenant General) Hanut Singh
34. Major (later Brigadier) Amarjit Singh Bal
35. Lieutenant Colonel (later Lieutenant General) Raj Mohan Vohra
36. Lieutenant Colonel (later Brigadier) RK Singh
37. Major DS Narang (Posthumous)
38. Subedar Malkiat Singh (Posthumous)
39. Lieutenant Colonel (later Major General) KL Rattan
40. Lieutenant Colonel (later Major General) Prem Kumar Khanna
41. Major (later Lieutenant Colonel) Jaivir Singh
42. Brigadier Mohinder Lal Whig
43. Colonel (later Brigadier) Udai Singh
44. Subedar (later Subedar Major) Mohinder Singh
45. Major (later Colonel) Chewang Rinchen, MVC and Bar
46. Captain Devinder Singh Ahlawat (Posthumous)
47. Lieutenant Colonel (later Brigadier) Narinder Singh Sandhu

48. Brigadier (later Lieutenant General) Krishnaswamy Gowri Shankar
49. Brigadier (later Major General) Anant Vishwanath Natu
50. Lieutenant Colonel (later Brigadier) Rattan Nath Sharma
51. Lieutenant Colonel (later Major General) Harish Chandra Pathak
52. Lance Naik Drig Pal Singh (Posthumous)
53. Sepoy Pandurang Salunkhe (Posthumous)
54. Major (later Colonel) Dharam Vir Singh
55. Rifleman Pati Ram Gurung (Posthumous)
56. Lance Naik (later Subedar Major) Nar Bahadur Chhetri
57. Assistant Commandant (BSF) Ram Krishna Wadhwa (Posthumous)

Air Force

58. Group Captain (later Air Vice Marshal) Chandan Singh
59. Wing Commander (later Air Vice Marshal) Vidya Bhushan Vashisht
60. Wing Commander (later Air Chief Marshal) Swaroop Krishna 'Suppi' Kaul
61. Wing Commander Padmanabha Gautam, MVC and Bar
62. Wing Commander (later Air Vice Marshal) Cecil Parker
63. Squadron Leader (later Air Marshal) Ravinder Nath Bhardwaj
64. Squadron Leader (later Air Vice Marshal) Madhabendra Banerji
65. Wing Commander (later Group Captain) Allan Albert D'Costa
66. Wing Commander (later Air Commodore) Ramesh Sakharam Benegal

67. Wing Commander (later Air Commodore) Harcharan Singh Mangat
68. Wing Commander (later Group Captain) Man Mohan Bir Singh Talwar

Navy

69. Captain Mahendra Nath Mulla (Posthumous)
70. Commander (later Commodore) Babru Bhan Yadav
71. Commander (later Commodore) KP Gopal Rao
72. Lieutenant Commander (later Rear Admiral) Santosh Kumar Gupta
73. Captain (later Vice Admiral) Swaraj Parkash
74. Commander (later Captain) Mohan NR Samant
75. Lieutenant Commander (later Commander) Joseph PA Noronha
76. Leading Seaman (later Petty Officer) Chiman Singh Yadav

Brig. Sant Singh, MVC and Bar

BRIG. Sant Singh—affectionately known as 'Sant Sipahi' or 'Saint Soldier'—was awarded his first Maha Vir Chakra during the 1965 India–Pakistan war. His exploits of valour during Operation 'Cactus Lily' in 1971 earned him the Bar to his MVC.

Born in 1921 into a marginal Jat Sikh farming family from Panjgrain Kalan in the princely state of Faridkot, he got enlisted in 1941 as a clerk in Faridkot State Forces Engineer Field Company. He was recommended by his British Commanding Officer for an Officer's Commission. After six years in the ranks, on 16 February 1947, Sant was commissioned into the 1st Battalion of the 14th Punjab Regiment as Emergency Commissioned Officer. During Partition, the regiment was allotted to Pakistan and Second Lieutenant Sant Singh was transferred to the 2nd Sikh Light Infantry battalion.

During the Junagarh operation in November 1947, as Intelligence Officer of the battalion, Second Lieutenant Sant Singh, at personal risk, provided vital information about the moves of the Junagarh forces that resulted in an almost bloodless takeover and smooth amalgamation of Junagarh into the Indian dominion.

As Lieutenant Colonel, he commanded the 5th Sikh Light Infantry from 1964 to 1968. It was during his command that in 1965 the battalion captured the heavily-defended Chuh-i-Nar feature on Balnoi ridge on 3 November 1965.

The feature dominated the LoC between Bhimber Gali, Mendhar and Balnoi in the Poonch sector, and its continued occupation by the Pakistan army would have resulted in total isolation of Balnoi from Mendhar and Krishna Ghati. Therefore, Chuh-i-Nar had to be captured at any cost.

For the daring capture, 5 Sikh Light Infantry earned two Maha Vir Chakras (including one for Sant Singh, the CO), one Vir Chakra and four Sena Medals.

Six years later, Brig. Sant Singh earned the Bar (award won the second time) to his MVC. On the outbreak of the 1971 war, he was commanding the newly created F-J Sector in the eastern theatre. He was tasked to advance towards Mymensingh on Haluaghat–Phulpur road. With a small fighting force (one infantry battalion, an engineer platoon and an artillery battery in direct support), the force captured some strongly held localities during the advance to Dhaka, reaching the outskirts by 13 December, further tightening the siege.

Brigadier Sant Singh, MVC, for his inspiring leadership and personal gallantry, was awarded the Bar to the Maha Vir Chakra he earned during the 1965 war. His citation reads:

During the 1971 India–Pakistan war, Brigadier Sant Singh, MVC, while commanding a sector on the eastern front, achieved spectacular results with a mixed force, having one regular battalion, advancing 38 miles almost on foot, to secure Mymensingh and Madhopur in eight days. During the advance, in spite of very stiff opposition from the enemy, he cleared heavily defended positions at several places. Throughout these actions, Brigadier Sant Singh, MVC, personally led and directed the troops, often exposing himself to enemy MMG fire and artillery shelling. His personal gallantry, leadership, skillful handling of meagre resources, audacity, improvisation and maximum use of local resources were responsible for the successful and rapid advance against the much stronger enemy in well prepared defensive positions.

Throughout, Brigadier Sant Singh, MVC, displayed conspicuous gallantry and inspiring leadership in keeping with the highest traditions of the Army.

Brig. Sant Singh retired in 1973 after a glorious military career spanning more than three decades. The war hero breathed his last on 9 December 2015.

The Tribune

Brig. Arun Sridhar Vaidya, MVC and Bar

O N a cold winter night, when his men in the tanks were still waiting to weave their way through fields where bombs could explode under their tracks, the Brigadier hustled from one machine to another. Stopping at the head of a column where a trawl tank was in the lead, he spoke a few words with another officer, a Sapper, on what the least risky path would be. There was no guarantee that least risky meant it would actually be safe. This would be the third minefield in a row. The semi-official history of the war would later record it as 1,460 yards wide.

General Arun Sridhar Vaidya rose to the very top, after being decorated with the same gallantry award twice—the first time in 1965 and the second time in 1971, earning him a Bar to the Maha Vir Chakra. He is one of only six soldiers to have got that distinction. He was assassinated in Pune in 1986 after he had retired.

Selected for the Armoured Corps from the Officers' Training School in Belgaum, he received an emergency commission in the Royal Deccan Horse (9th Deccan Horse) on 20 January 1947 and regular commission on 7 May that year.

As the officer commanding the 16th (Independent) Armoured Brigade in 1971, he was deployed with the 54 Infantry Division. In the words of the Pakistani military analyst, Maj Agha Humayun Amin (retd), 'The toughest battles of the 1971 war were fought opposite the (Indian) 54 Infantry Division.'

The Division was tasked in the 1 Corps area of responsibility immediately north of the Shakargarh bulge, the protrusion of the Pakistani territory that, at its easternmost tip, threatened the national highway between Pathankot and Jammu linking to Kashmir. Vaidya's brigade launched from the general area of Mawa–Galar on the banks of the Degh river and heading south went on to establish a bridgehead and expand it across the Basantar in the face of fierce counter-attacks.

The many battles and skirmishes in the Shakargarh sector are rich with overwhelming tales of gallantry—and the one that stands out the most is that of Second Lt Arun Khetarpal (who was posthumously awarded the Param Vir Chakra), the Poona Horse officer in Vaidya's brigade in the Battle of Basantar. But before that dramatic tank-versus-tank shootout, Brigadier Vaidya had already been briefed by his divisional commander, Maj. Gen. (later Lt Gen.) Walter Antony Gustavo ('Wag') Pinto, that his regiments would be in two thrusts towards the Pakistani defences on the Zafarwal–Dhamtal line.

To some extent, the penetrations by the 54 Division were prompted by a tardy response from the 36 Division in the south of the Shakargarh bulge. The 54 Division's route was planned to be between the Basantar and Karir rivers. The advance began on the night of 5/6 December. Pakistan had laid at least three lines of minefields. The anti-tank mines were densely laid, with one estimate that there was a mine every three to five feet. The minefields had to be cleared for Indian tanks and troops to reach their objectives, among which were Barapind–Jarpal. Vaidya was told that he, along with the 9th Engineers, whose Commanding Officer was Lt Col BT Pandit, would have to take the responsibility for the trawling and clearing.

'The battles of Karir N (nullah) crossing at Chakra and the crossing of Basantar N at Sarajchak will go down in history as epoch-making deliberate mine-breach operations against well-fortified enemy positions by well-knit teams of all arms: infantry, engineers, armour and artillery,' Pinto would write later in his special order of the day. One officer wrote in a light-hearted reminiscence that the operation was akin to 'breaking through a metal cage buried miles deep in the earth.' In modern military terms, though, it was slow and painstaking, despite the Division's later posters put up inside Pakistan that read 'Bash on, regardless.'

To the east of the Zafarwal–Dhamtal line, at Dehira and Chakra, the advancing forces were met with heavy opposition, not only from the mines, but also from fortified infantry positions with concrete bunkers. In a later introspection, Pakistani officers said it was a blunder on the part of Pakistan's 1 Corps that was defending to not take advantage of the fact that the Indian thrust was 'fixed' between the first and second layers of minefields.

General Vaidya, who was battle-hardened from the Burma campaign in World War II and the 1965 war, which was more of a stalemate, personally swung between the two arms of the 54 Division, encouraging his men, with he himself trawling through. He was seen peering through binoculars, surveying the field from Centurion tanks, often accompanied by men of 9 Engineers, also called 'Thambis' because they comprised mostly Tamil-speaking troops. In one axis, the columns had to go through six minefields, one of them in the riverbed of the Basantar, totalling 8,000 yards (about 7.3 km) in length. They had been fed some intelligence from East Pakistan troops who had defected. But much of it was outdated.

The citation for the Bar to Vaidya's MVC reads:

In the battle of Chakra and Dehira, the going was difficult due to deep minefield and terrain. In a cool and confident manner, Brigadier Vaidya undertook the crossing through the minefield. He personally moved forward, disregarding personal safety.

Through his inspired leadership, the entire squadron pushed through the lane and quickly deployed itself to meet the enemy's counter-attacks. During the Battle of Basantar, he again displayed his professional skill and superb leadership. He got his tanks through one of the deepest minefields, expanded the bridgehead and repulsed a strong enemy counter-attack. In this battle, 62 enemy tanks were destroyed.

In the fields around, the trees were charred from the shelling and the stink from the carcasses of animals in the deserted little villages of mud houses hung heavy. But the Indian forces of the 54 Division had advanced eight-to-thirteen km into Pakistan.

When the ceasefire was accepted on the western front on 17 December—Dhaka having already fallen, and the Pakistan forces under Niazi having surrendered the previous day—Vaidya and his men were in sight of Zafarwal but had not reached their initial objectives. That was estimated to take four to five days from the day the operations were launched: dusk on 5 December. The Division was to breach the Zafarwal–Dhamtal line and then go for Deoli and Mirzapur.

Even though the western front for India in 1971 was mostly a 'holding operation', Vaidya was in the thick of the bloodiest battles that continue to hold lessons for integrated operations to this day. The battles also threw up heroes on both sides.

'There were also other acts of bravery and determination,' noted *The Tribune*'s unnamed reporter in a dispatch 'from the Basantar banks' days later. 'A little away from Zafarwal, a Major from Haryana insisted on staying on his job till his Brigadier affectionately ordered his immediate removal for treatment,' the reporter added.

Sujan Dutta

Brig. Kailash Prasad Pande

KAILASH Prasad Pande, who was from Gwalior, came from a family with a tradition of sending sons into the Army. Pande was commissioned into the Gwalior State Forces on 25 August 1945. After the princely states amalgamated with the Indian dominion, Pande, a subaltern, joined 42 Field Regiment. In 1964, Lt Col Pande, affectionately called 'Tom', raised and also commanded 56 Mountain Composite Regiment (Pack).

Promoted to the rank of Brigadier in 1970, he was given the command of 2 Mountain Artillery Brigade deployed in Arunachal Pradesh on the border with Bhutan, Tibet and Burma.

In the early stages of Operation 'Cactus Lily', the battle to capture the Dhalai post saw fierce fighting. Brig Shiv Yadav, Commander of 61 Mountain Brigade, was badly injured, and Lt Gen. Sagat Singh, Corps Commander of 4 Corps, gave charge to Brig. Pande, who was functioning as artillery adviser to the divisional commander.

After regrouping and planning afresh, the battle recommenced. The fiercely-fought battle saw Brig. Pande leading from the front. After the successful operation, he was directed to take over the brigade formally. Under his leadership, 61 Mountain Brigade accomplished several difficult tasks as it advanced 40 miles in just three days. On 9 December, Brig. Pande advanced alongside 12 Kumaon and a troop of armour, and ensured that Daudkandi, a vital communication centre south-east of Dacca, was secured by the last light. Nearly 1,500 Pakistanis were captured. On 16 December, Brig. Sheikh Mansoor Hussain Attif, Commander of Pakistan's 117 Infantry Brigade, surrendered to Brig. Pande, along with 5,000 troops.

Brig Pande was awarded the Maha Vir Chakra. His citation reads:

> 61 Mountain Brigade, commanded by Brigadier Kailash Prasad Pande, was assigned the task of clearing a well-fortified position in the eastern theatre in December 1971. The task was successfully completed mainly due to Brigadier Pande's inspiring leadership. He was always well forward, unmindful of his safety, encouraging troops and directing the battle. His brigade group advanced 40 miles in 72 hours, effectively bottling up the enemy and capturing the key posts. When lodgement was attained in the fortress of Mynamati defences, his brigade was subjected to the determined enemy attacks supported by tanks. Against all the relentless pressure of the enemy, the brigade held onto the defences until surrender by the enemy commander.

Throughout the operations, Brigadier Pande displayed gallantry, leadership and devotion to duty of a high order for which he was awarded the Maha Vir Chakra.

After the liberation of Bangladesh, while the Indian Army was promptly withdrawn, 61 Mountain Brigade was told to stay on. For eight months, 61, now a Mountain Brigade Group, under the command of Brig. Pande, helped put down rebellions and near uprisings, especially in the Chittagong Hill tracts.

Brig Kailash Prasad 'Tom' Pande, MVC, retired in 1979 and settled down in Bhopal. He breathed his last on 4 February 2010, while attending the artillery reunion at the School of Artillery, Deolali. By his side was General Deepak Kapoor, his son-in-law.

The Tribune

Lt Col Kulwant Singh Pannu

FABRIC is synonymous with the name of Tangail. The warp and weft of the Tangail saree is known in every Bengali home and in the wider world of women who drape the garment. Whether it is cotton or silk or a mix of the two, the Tangail saree, known for its plain body and rich border, handloomed by generations of weavers, is now generic.

Fabric covered the skies over Tangail, the town the saree is named after, 90-odd km north-west of Dhaka in the early evening of 11 December 1971. Ripstop nylon billowed like domes of military green as Indian soldiers of the 2 Para battalion group made what remains the only airborne operation of its kind led by a commander who was the first out of an IAF cargo plane with his jeep.

In three days, Lt Col Kulwant Singh Pannu, later Major General, would also walk into the Dacca International Hotel.

After a wash, the 'flamboyant Commanding Officer of 2 Para spoke to reporters', according to military historian Arjun Subramaniam, who has seen the unit's archives. The hotel was designated a safe zone by the UN and the Red Cross.

Two days later, Pannu would also bound off his jeep after parking it in the grounds of the headquarters of Pakistan's Eastern Command, brush past a stern sentry with his adjutant Capt. Nirbhay Sharma and the Bangladesh Mukti Bahini leading light Kader 'Tiger' Siddiqui, and hand over to AAK Niazi a message from General Nagra: 'Abdullah,' it said, 'it's game over, surrender.'

In the time that it took to jump out of the IAF C-119 'Packet' and park the jeep in Dhaka Cantonment, Lt Col Pannu and his men had passed into legend, their exploits forever to feature in texts studied by professional soldiers.

'I was returning to Tangail from one of our headquarters at Mohanandapur village when the Indian Army paratroopers started landing near Poongli,' wrote Anwarul Ham, a former ambassador and then second-in-command of the Mukti Bahini in Tangail.

> It was quite a sight. I was 1.5 miles away and I ran to greet them. I introduced myself to Lt Col Pannu. He made two requests: to disperse the crowd of villagers (who were gawking) and to arrange for local volunteers to help carry the load and push the artillery guns and jeeps to the road.

Three of the four guns had fallen into ponds. One landed on the roof of a village house. The battalion group that had landed comprised elements of a field battery and medics. The drop was spread over a wide area, by one estimate over 20 sq. km. The battalion was tasked with securing the Poongli bridge and the adjacent ferry on the Louhajang river that branched from the wide Jamuna. Securing the bridge would cut off the battalions of Pakistan's 93 Brigade that were falling back to Tangail and Dhaka from Mymensingh and Jamalpur. The Indian operation was deep behind enemy lines, the battalion group having flown in from Kalaikunda and Dum Dum in West Bengal. They had linked up with 1 Maratha Light Infantry, who were already in the thick of operations, battling their way through East Pakistan from Tura in Meghalaya.

To fulfil his brief, Pannu had to rally round his men and equipment, moving in a wide arc as night fell. Having rounded up a bulk of his men, he prepared to take the bridge. Four artillery guns could be made operational for the charge. Most of the Pakistanis fled, but that same night, there were three counter-attacks on Poongli bridge.

'I came face to face with bone-chilling scenes of last night's battle. Corpses of hundreds of enemy soldiers littered the road, bodies from one side of the bridge to another. We walked with care so as to not step on the dead,' wrote Dr Nuran Nabi, a lieutenant of Tiger Siddiqui's force in Dhaka's *Daily Star*, some thirty years after the event.

The 2 Para group, having linked up with 1 Maratha Light Infantry, then rolled cautiously towards Dhaka on the Mirzapur–Jaydebpur road, reaching Milestone 26, its destination, by the evening of 15 December. They were then tasked to turn west and reach Dhaka through the Mirpur bridge. The bridge was staunchly defended, even though by 15 December, the war was collapsing for Pakistan.

'We lost three—killed in action. There were forty-one enemy casualties but we were at the gates of Dhaka by midnight,' Nirbhay Sharma, who was adjutant to Pannu and who retired as a Lieutenant General (and then became Governor of Arunachal and Mizoram), has written and said in many interviews.

The next day, Pannu, Sharma and Tiger Siddiqui were to take the message to Niazi. Pannu, who had tied up with Tiger Siddiqui after the airdrop in Tangail, had taken him along on the battles all the way to Dhaka. He wanted him along not only for the camaraderie they had struck up, but also because of the clear idea drilled into Indian officers that this was not a country they were to occupy but were here only to help the Mukti Bahini.

Such was fate, however, for the men who fought alongside that Tiger Siddiqui had to be arrested by the Indian Army in later weeks for having publicly bayoneted surrendered Razakars (Pakistan's collaborators) personally in the cricket stadium in Dhaka, an incident that was filmed.

Before the Indian Army's entry into the Dhaka cantonment, however, the Indian Army's Eastern Command Chief of Staff, Maj. Gen. JFR Jacob, had proclaimed from Calcutta that Indian paratroopers had surrounded the East Pakistan capital. Even if it was an overstatement, it carried weight because by that time, Lt General Sagat Singh's forces from the east had crossed the Meghna river.

The 2 Paras led by Pannu were among the first to actually march into Dhaka and extract that famous confession from Niazi. Niazi could not meet Pannu's gaze, wrote Nirbhay Sharma. He was unshaven—*'Pindi mein baithe haramzadon ne marwa diya.* (expletive ... people in Rawalpindi, Pakistan's

General Headquarters, have betrayed me with false promises of help).'

The remarkable thing about Pannu's leadership was that the Indian Army had only one officer with personal experience of an airborne operation till then: Lt Gen. Inder Singh Gill, who as a Lieutenant was a commando in Greece for the Allied Forces in 1942. He was Director of Military Operations at the Army Headquarters in 1971.

Lt Col KS Pannu's MVC citation reads:

Lieutenant Colonel KS Pannu was commanding a battalion, which was airdropped near Tangail on December 11, 1971. The task involved cutting enemy routes of withdrawal and preventing his build-up at Tangail. This also involved the capture of an enemy position on a vital bridge at Poongli. The drop of the battalion was widely dispersed and Lieutenant Colonel Pannu had to move from one location to another under enemy fire to collect his platoons. It was entirely due to his cool courage, utter disregard for his personal safety and his timely and skilful direction that his battalion captured the enemy position at Poongli.

Under his able leadership, the battalion repulsed numerous counter-attacks, inflicting heavy casualties on the enemy. Lieutenant Colonel Pannu displayed conspicuous gallantry, exemplary leadership, determination and devotion to duty in keeping with the best traditions of the Army.

Sujan Dutta

Maj. Kuldip Singh Chandpuri

THE family's genes of valour were tempered in World War I, reinforced during World War II, and decorated in the third generation at Longewala. Karam Singh served with XXXVI Sikhs (Saragarhi Battalion) in Mesopotamia in World War I, and his son Wattan Singh served in St John's Ambulance Brigade during World War II.

Karam Singh decided to move the family from a rain-dependent farming area to canal-irrigated fertile lands that he had invested in. In early 1938, the family left Chandpur Rurki village (7 kms from Garhshankar) for Chak 161/9L in Montgomery district (now in Pakistan). It was here that Kuldip Singh was born, on 22 November 1940; his two sisters followed. Things were beginning to look up, but providence had other plans. A young seven-year-old saw the horrors of Partition; he, along with his mother and sisters, were evacuated by the Army to Amritsar, where Col Assa Singh, a family friend, provided shelter. The male members had to trudge back in different groups, avoiding murdering marauders. The family reunited at Chandpur Rurki.

Football had caught young Kuldip's fancy. After passing high school from Saroya, football took him to SGS Khalsa College, Mahilpur, which was considered a nursery of the game, and then to Government College, Hoshiarpur. While still doing his graduation, he became an under officer in National Cadet Corps (NCC), participating in the Republic Day Parade of 1962. Later the same year, the Chinese invasion took place. At about this time, Punjab Chief Minister Partap Singh Kairon visited the college, seeking volunteers to fight the nation's enemies. Kuldip Singh joined the Officers Training Academy, Madras, passing out in 1963. Second Lt Kuldip Singh Chandpuri joined the 3rd Battalion of the Punjab Regiment.

Soon, the India–Pakistan 1965 war took place and 3 Punjab was defending the Beas bridge as the enemy's armour thrust threatened to cut off a major chunk of Punjab. Being a reserve battalion, 3 Punjab saw frequent changes in tasks and locations, all adding to the experience of Lt Chandpuri. The same year, the battalion moved for its UN Mission assignment in Gaza for a year.

In May 1971, Capt. Chandpuri was posted to 23 Punjab, then located at Bikaner with an operational role in the Jaisalmer sector. Maj. Chandpuri, after his promotion, was assigned the command of the Alfa (Sikh) Company. Punjab battalions have a mix of two Sikh and two Dogra companies. Soon, Maj. Chandpuri was detailed for a month-long familiarization with the operational area, which was to pay great dividends in the war that was to follow.

Anticipating the war, 23 Punjab had occupied its battle positions. Maj. Chandpuri's Alfa Company was defending Longewala, the sweet water position, while the remaining battalion was occupying a defended area at Sadewala. The remaining brigade was at Tanot. The Longewala position was reasonably well fortified with anti-tank mines laid by the Pioneer section, largely towards the south-west. The only wire fence that circumvented the position was basically laid to keep out the wild camels that came sniffing for water. This wire was to prove the undoing of the attackers.

A section each of 81-mm mortars, 7.62-mm MMG and 106-mm recoil-less rifles (RCLs) were in location. Having patrolled the areas around and fortified the trenches, the Punjabis were confident of themselves. Intelligence inputs pointed to a Pakistani attack, and sure enough, on 3 December, air strikes on all Indian airfields announced the start of the war on the western front. On the night of 4–5 December, Lt Dharamvir, Company Officer with Maj. Chandpuri, reported large columns of tanks and infantry moving towards Longewala. Maj. Chandpuri collected his men, spoke to them about their rich martial traditions, and urged them to hold fast at all costs. He, however, said that anyone who feared death was free to leave, but he would fight to the very last. '*Loon deh mull chakon da wayla agaya sathiyo* (the time has come to repay a national debt),' he said.

A series of 'jaikaras' of '*Jo Bole So Nihal, Sat Sri Akal*' reverberated in the air as Maj. Chandpuri realized that his motivational tirade had hit home. His request for reinforcement and tanks was still pending with his CO when the enemy tanks closed in on the wire and gradually spread out to surround the post. Exchange of small arms fire had commenced, and with that, all avenues of reinforcement were now blocked. Maj. Chandpuri expected a tank assault on his weak defence any time. Fortunately, that did not happen. The enemy tanks, taking the cattle fence to be a minefield, halted. The infantry started shooting on the Punjabi defences. The wire had successfully separated the infantry from its tank support. The battle was now between an infantry battalion and the resolute Alfa Company of 23 Punjab.

The 106 RCL gun of Maj. Chandpuri now got into action, the first round scoring a hit against a T-59 tank that had closed in, which soon burst into flames. The second RCL gun knocked out an enemy jeep. Seeing the result, the MMG and 81-mm mortars opened fire, imposing further caution on the enemy infantry accompanying the tanks. At this juncture, Sepoy Bishan Das of Pioneer Platoon, on orders, began to place anti-tank mines on the likely routes of the tanks.

Maj. Chandpuri, in order to motivate his men, moved from trench to trench under enemy fire. Tank-tracer rounds were guiding every fire and making it more accurate; men were getting injured, but seeing their company commander moving under fire kept the company motivated.

As day broke, the IAF Hunter aircraft took to the air, targeting every tank in the open. Initially, the aircraft avoided engaging tanks very close to the Company locality, thinking them to be India's own. But once the ground reality was communicated, every tank was shot. Early on 5 December, Lt Dharamvir's patrol had reinforced the company, along with three Amx-13 tanks of the Independent Squadron.

Longewala Company had held the better part of the enemy brigade and a tank regiment on the basis of sheer willpower. The IAF than went into a happy shooting mode, making the

Longewala area a graveyard of enemy tanks; thirty-seven were destroyed, breaking the back of the Pakistani offensive to capture Jaisalmer.

For his conspicuous gallantry and inspiring leadership, Maj. KS Chandpuri was awarded the Maha Vir Chakra. Kuldeep Singh Chandpuri, MVC, rose to the rank of Brigadier and was also Commandant of the Punjab Regimental Centre. He also became an international referee in athletics. He breathed his last on 17 November 2018 at Chandigarh, leaving behind a rich legacy.

Brig. IS Gakhal (Retd)

Brig. Hardev Singh Kler

BRIG. Hardev Singh Kler was among the seven Brigadier-ranked officers who were awarded the Maha Vir Chakra in the 1971 war on the eastern front. Kler was a third-generation soldier from Kakrala Kalan near Ludhiana. His father, Capt. Chhajja Singh, had earned the Order of British India during World War II. Hardev, Captain Chhajja Singh's second son, earned the Ati Vishisht Seva Medal in the 1965 India–Pakistan war and the Maha Vir Chakra during Operation 'Cactus Lily' in 1971.

Hardev was commissioned into the Corps of Signals in 1943. At nineteen, he was the youngest Indian to have been commissioned into the British Indian Army. He was given an option to get seconded to the elite Paratroopers Brigade, but Capt. Hardev declined the option, choosing to be a Signalman like his father.

Lt Col Hardev Singh Kler, for his distinguished wartime services rendered during 'Operation Gibraltar' in 1965, was awarded the Ati Vishisht Seva Medal (AVSM), a rare honour for a Lt Col.

In the 1971 war, Brig. Hardev Singh Kler, while commanding 95 Mountain Brigade in the eastern theatre, led the advance with Dhaka as the terminal objective. By 8 December, the brigade had contacted Jamalpur, strongly held by Pakistan's 93 Infantry Brigade. Jamalpur, though encircled, held on even after Lt Col Sultan, head of Jamalpur Garrison, was told to surrender. The reply by the Pakistani officer showed that though the chips were down, the morale of the Pakistani commanders was high.

However, Col Sultan was unaware that 95 Mountain Brigade Group was sitting behind him south of Jamalpur. During the final assault by 1 Maratha Light Infantry, Brig. Kler advanced, along with the forward platoon. On the night of 10–11 December, Col Sultan, along with Brig. Abdul Qadir Khan, Commander of 93 Pakistan Infantry Brigade, together with 31 Baluch, pulled out of Jamalpur and took defences at Tangail, 9 km in the rear.

In recognition of his bold planning, execution and conspicuous bravery, Brig Hardev Singh Kler was awarded the Maha Vir Chakra. His citation reads:

Brigadier Hardev Singh Kler, AVSM, was commanding a mountain brigade on the eastern front. He led the advance of his brigade from Jamalpur up to Turag river. During all the actions in the advance, Brig. Kler was personally present with the leading troops and directed the operations with complete disregard to his life. By personally going into the thick of the battle, he provided great inspiration to his troops who had laid siege behind enemy positions south of Jamalpur. Under his command, the brigade inflicted heavy casualties on the enemy and captured 379 prisoners as well as large quantities of weapons and ammunition.

Incidentally, his son, Flight Lt DJS Kler, also fought in the war in the eastern theatre and in the same sector.

The Tribune

Brig. Anand Sarup

SON of a Viceroy Commissioned Officer (present-day Junior Commissioned Officer), Anand Sarup aspired to be an Indian Commissioned Officer. After his Senior Cambridge from King George's Royal Military College, Jalandhar, he cleared the IMA selection process and was commissioned into 8 Gorkha Rifles in 1949.

Just prior to the 1971 war, Brigadier Anand Sarup, Commandant of the Counter Insurgency & Jungle Warfare School in Mizoram, was given command of an ad hoc establishment named 'Kilo Force'. It had been created with two regular modified infantry battalions (31 Jat and 32 Mahar, present-day 12 Jat and 15 Mahar) from Mizo Hills, 4th and 10th East Bengal Battalions, 92nd Border Security Force (BSF) battalion, one Central Reserve Police Force (CRPF) battalion, one Mukti Fauj battalion, an artillery mountain regiment, Mujib artillery battery, and a BSF Post Group.

Within a fortnight of the raising of the force, 5,000 to 6,000 men were welded into a cohesive fighting force. At the outbreak of the war, the 'K' force was launched into the battle from its firm base in Mizoram near the East Pakistan border.

After the declaration of the war on 3 December, Kilo Force won hard-fought skirmishes, but the pursuit got stalled at Feni town, strongly defended by two enemy companies. Feni was a tactically important road and rail route to Chittagong harbour, and needed to be captured to cut off the harbour from the rest of East Pakistan.

Based on a reconnaissance report, Brig. Sarup came up with a bold plan, and by December 6, Feni was captured. Also captured were Karrehat and Zorarganj. To speed up the capture of Chittagong, Kilo Force was reinforced with 83 Mountain Brigade under the overall command of Brig. Sarup. Kilo Force reached Faujdahat on the outskirts of Chittagong on the night of 13–14 December, when operations were suspended. At Faujdahat, the force captured almost a battalion size of prisoners of war.

Brig. Sarup was awarded the Maha Vir Chakra. His citation reads:

> Brigadier Anand Sarup was allotted the task of organising and launching into battle an ad hoc force for engaging the enemy at Pathanagar and in the area north of Feni town in eastern theatre. He organised and trained this force in a very short period and the troops under his command fought gallantly during the battles at Feni, Nazirhat, Kumarighat and Faujdahat. During the operations, Brig

Sarup was constantly on the move, well forward with his troops, directing the operations. Under his leadership, the capture of Feni isolated the Chittagong harbour, which negated the war effort of Pakistan to a great extent. Capture of strongly held Kumarighat defended locality was truly the hallmark of the bold and innovative planning by Brig Sarup and equally bold execution by the troops under his command.

The Tribune

Lt Col Sawai Bhawani Singh and Lt Col Sukhjit Singh

SO much champagne flowed to celebrate his birth, as myth and legend have it, that they nicknamed him 'Bubbles'.

It was not a Champagne Run, though, that got 'Brigadier His Highness Saramad-i-Rajahai Hindustan Raj Rajendra Shri Maharajadhiraj Sawai Bhawani Singh Bahadur' a Maha Vir Chakra when he was a Lieutenant Colonel in 1971.

For, the last of the 'Maharajas'—before Prime Minister Indira Gandhi abolished the privy purse for the rulers of the erstwhile princely states in India earlier that year—was lionized for having led raid after raid at the head of 10 Paras (commandos).

Later to be known as the 10 Para Special Forces ('Desert Scorpions'), the battalion was the tip of the spear that pierced deep into the enemy territory in Pakistan's Sindh through the

Thar desert, in a territory that was once partly under the House of Kacchawaha (the Jaipur royals).

The citation by the Ministry of Defence for Lt Col Bhawani Singh reads:

> On the night of December 5 (1971), Lt Colonel Sawai Bhawani Singh, who was commanding a battalion of the Parachute Regiment (commandos), led his men deep into the enemy territory and for four days and nights, with complete disregard for his personal safety, made skilful and relentless raids on the strongly held posts at Chachro and Virawah.

There were two companies Lt Col Bhawani Singh was leading— Alpha and Charlie. After zooming through the night over sandy desert dunes and vales in Jongas, the companies scared the enemy, first with the cacophony they caused. Then, Alpha company partly surrounded a wing of the Pakistani Rangers' fortified post at Chachro, some 70 km from the border, while Charlie company raided it. They took prisoners.

Then the commandos headed for Virawah. The earlier action repeated itself, with the element of hand-to-hand fighting added. In 'gingering up the enemy', Bhawani Singh's boys killed seventeen Pakistani soldiers in the surgical strikes with light machine guns mounted on their jeeps. Then they raided Nagarparkar, another defended Pakistani position, before returning to the base. At the base, they were given yet another task—to blow up an ammo dump in Islamkot, which they duly proceeded to do. Every one of them returned from each one of those raids. There was no Indian casualty. At last count, thirty-six Pakistani soldiers were killed by the Paras and twenty-two were taken prisoners.

In the blitzkrieg that was said to have been modelled after a British SAS raid behind German lines in Libya during World War II, there was a dissonance between one version, 'A', which was anecdotal, and another, 'B', which was the formally recorded version of events.

In 'A' (accounts publicly available and promoted by the Jaipur royals), Lt Col Bhawani Singh, after crossing into the Pakistani territory, came across the local Khemkhanis (Rajput Muslims), who had learnt that their maharaja was in the vicinity and wanted to pay obeisance to him. According to a written account by his friend Brigadier Sukhjit Singh, they were eager to reverentially bow to him, with cries of 'Khama Ghani Maharaj'. The villagers, according to Sukhjit Singh, were 'demonstrating that borders have never severed generational ties of fealty'.

'B' is actually non-existent now, as there is no battle action report or citations of 10 Para SF during 1971, according to the Ministry of Defence. The response to a Right to Information query on the records said, 'The relevant record of citations has been destroyed as per policy in vogue' (as reported by *The Print* in 2019).

'The name "Bubbles" is in a way a misnomer for the frivolity it implies,' Sukhjit Singh wrote evocatively after his friend's death in April 2011.

> He was not an indolent prince of leisure but an exemplar tour de force, who brought gravitas to each and every one of his roles and responsibilities. At the same time, it should be conceded that his effervescent personality gave ample grounds for this to be a well-suited "pet name". Military punctilio, ceremonial exactitude and elegance, all came naturally to him.

Sukhjit Singh is a prince himself, from the House of Kapurthala. His fondest memory is of rides with his grandfather, the Maharaja of Kapurthala, 'in a zebra-driven chariot in the zoological gardens of the palace', according to an interview he gave to *The Tribune*.

Sukhjit Singh, also of the armoured corps' Scinde Horse (14 Horse), was its Commanding Officer as a Lieutenant Colonel in the Shakargarh sector, the bulge that threatened the Pathankot–Jammu national highway linking to Srinagar.

His exploits with his men on the T-55 tanks—modern at that time—are part of military lore to this day. The Scinde Horse was the first regiment to have got tanks imported from Soviet Russia in 1966.

Sukhjit Singh was leading the charge from the south of the bulge, in skirmishes leading to the epic Battle of Basantar. 'On December 10, 1971, his regiment was deployed west of Naina Kot when the enemy launched an armoured attack in strength under cover of intense artillery and heavy mortar fire,' his citation noted.

Despite the flak from the Pakistani forces, Sukhjit Singh manoeuvred his machines, leading his columns from the open cupola of his own tank, sometimes with his dust goggles raised to the forehead to see better through binoculars so that he could direct volleys from his men most effectively.

The next day, on 11 December, again he personally outflanked the enemy to close in on them, despite its medium artillery and mortar fire. The Pakistanis lost eight tanks, Shermans and Pattons. The intention was to capture the enemy tanks. One Pakistani officer, two junior commissioned officers and two other ranks were taken prisoner at Malakpur.

Sukhjit Singh was already a veteran of armoured warfare, having been schooled in this domain while serving with the

Armoured Division in the Sialkot sector during the 1965 operations.

An excerpt from *The Tribune* of 19 March 2021 quoting him reads:

> The 1971 war was raging. I was Lieut Col at that time. My troops managed to round up Pakistani soldiers. Among them was a tall, smart guy with whom I began talking just to cull more information. As our conversation was on, he told me, "I have one last wish." I replied, "What makes you think that we are going to kill you?" During further inquiry, we got to know that he is the son of Sikandar Hayat Khan, a former premier of Punjab. He was among those who were set free. Much later, I met the family as well.

After twenty-six years in the Army and the decoration, the man who led that charge is said to have influenced former Punjab Chief Minister Capt. Amarinder Singh (of the Patiala royals) to join the Army.

Sawai Bhawani Singh and Sukhjit Singh were not only contemporaries in service, but they were also friends outside the military. Bhawani Singh was schooled at Sheshbagh in Srinagar, Doon and Harrow. He was commissioned in the 3rd Cavalry in 1951 before he moved to the President's Bodyguard and then to 10 Paras. He was recalled to service to be conferred the rank of Brigadier post-retirement and was sent out on diplomatic assignments afterwards.

Sukhjit Singh was also educated at Doon School before training at the IMA.

Sujan Dutta

Maj. BS Mankotia

THE Indian enclave at Ranian, south-east of the Ravi-international border confluence, was designated as the vital ground to be held at all costs. During the 1971 war, the Pakistan army was desperate to capture Ranian, which could facilitate their advance to Amritsar. The 9 Punjab, supported by a squadron of tanks, was tasked with denying Pakistan ingress into Ranian.

During the fifteen-day war, 'C' Company of 9 Punjab, under the command of Maj. Basdev Singh Mankotia, not only blunted the repeated enemy attacks on Ranian, but also captured Pakistan territory before the declaration of ceasefire on 17 December. At the helm was Basdev Singh, a Himachali Dogra from Sidhpurgarh village in the present-day Kangra district.

Maj. Mankotia, for his conspicuous act of gallantry, was awarded the Maha Vir Chakra. His citation reads:

Major Basdev Singh Mankotia of the 9th Punjab Battalion was holding a screen position with his company between Ranian and the International Border with Pakistan. Between 4th and 5th December, Pakistan's 18 Frontier Force attacked his position seven times, all the time supported by the armour. With Major Mankotia in the forefront inspiring his men to hold firm, all the attacks were repulsed with heavy casualties on the attackers. When a portion of the screen position was over-run by the enemy, Major Mankotia hastily organised his men and led a determined counter-attack from the left flank on the cry *'Durge Mata ki Jai'* and regained the lost ground, although at a cost.

During the successful counter-attack, he was seriously wounded in both the shoulders but seeing the importance of regaining the ground, he refused to get evacuated and continued inspiring and leading his men till the enemy was completely driven out of the screen position.

The Tribune

Lance Naik Shangara Singh
(Posthumous)

ON a high ground close to GT road and the international border, Pulkanjri village in Amritsar district was held by the BSF Company Headquarters before the start of the war. On 3 December, when Pakistan launched surprise attacks all along the western border, the BSF elements from Pulkanjri BOP were withdrawn overnight since the feature was not considered defensible. Militarily, Pakistan needed the feature, and on the night of 4 December, its 15th Punjab battalion simply extracted it for the country.

Pulkanjri was located within the territorial jurisdiction of 2 Sikh, which decided to recapture it at the earliest. The battle to recapture Pulkanjri was among the fiercest fought and decisively won on the western front in the 1971 war.

A lightning commando raid was planned by a platoon strength of men to be led by Capt. PS Toor. The much-awaited order to recapture Pulkanjri came at 5.45 p.m. on 17 December, with just a couple of hours remaining for the unilateral ceasefire to be effective. A quick counter-attack plan was made and artillery fire plan was coordinated. 'C' Company, under the command of Maj. Narain Singh Koak, was given the task of recapturing Pulkanjri before first light the next day.

After half an hour of bombardment by Pakistan, the attack began at 7 p.m. The attackers, out in the open despite all odds stacked against them, kept charging under covering fire from the guns of 175 Field Regiment and the battalion's 3-inch mortars under Capt Toor. Just when the men were 200 yards short of the objective, two medium machine guns of the enemy opened up with devastating fire.

At that critical juncture, Lance Naik Shangara Singh, in a rare display of courage, albeit at the highest cost, silenced both the machine guns, paving the way for his platoon to charge and drag the enemy out from the bunkers.

Hailing from Chohla Sahib in Amritsar district, Shangara had been enrolled in 2 Sikh in 1964. He was awarded the Maha Vir Chakra. His citation reads:

On December 17, 1971, Lance Naik Shangara Singh of 2nd Sikh Battalion was Second-in-Command of a section in the forward platoon during the attack on Pulkanjri village. While closing onto the objective, the platoon in which he was serving came under heavy enemy fire, particularly from two machine guns on the east flank. Many jawans fell and the attack could not proceed further.

To save the life of his comrades as also to maintain the momentum of the attack, Shangara, with utter disregard for personal safety, made a dash through the minefield to the first machine gun post and hurled a grenade inside the bunker, successfully silencing the machine gun. Then he charged toward the second machine gun post, leapt over the loophole and succeeded in physically snatching the gun. In doing so, he received a burst of fire in his abdomen, but undeterred, he continued to hold the machine gun. The enemy was completely unnerved and the firing crew fled from the bunker, leaving the machine gun barrel in Shangara's hands.

Elimination of these two machine guns enabled the platoon to dash forward and take on the enemy in fierce hand-to-hand combat. The hard slogging match continued for over an hour after which the enemy withdrew leaving behind its dead and wounded. Immediately, Shangara was pulled back for evacuation; however, due to excessive loss of blood, he succumbed to his injuries.

The Tribune

Sepoy Anusuya Prasad
(Posthumous)

ONE of the youngest MVC awardees, Sepoy Anusuya Prasad was recruited into the Mahar Regiment on 19 May 1971, the day he turned eighteen. Prasad was from the village of Channa in Uttar Pradesh's Chamoli district (now in Uttarakhand). He was sent to the Mahar Regimental Centre at Sagar (MP) for the mandatory nine months' training. He got married during the training break to Chitra, who was then in her early teens.

With the war imminent, the drafts at all regimental centres were sent to their respective battalions. And so, Anusuya Prasad joined 'C' Company of 10 Mahar on 20 November at Shamsher Nagar in the eastern bulge of East Pakistan. As fate would have it, he died fighting within ten days of commencement of action, but not before making his country and battalion proud.

A company each of 22 Baluch and 91 Mujahid Battalion of the Pakistan army held on to the heavily fortified tea factory on the outskirts of Maulvi Bazaar. The 10 Mahar made two robust attempts to get through, but these were foiled by heavy automatic fire from the house of the factory manager, and the casualty figure was high.

That is when Sepoy Prasad, in a rare display of courage, set the entire building afire, paving the way for his battalion to capture the tea factory on 30 November, three days before the declaration of war.

His MVC citation reads:

Sepoy Anusuya Prasad of the 10th Battalion, the Mahar Regiment, was a young soldier who had joined the unit on November 20, 1971. On November 29, his battalion was given the task of capturing Maulvi Bazaar defended locality as a part of our offensive on the eastern front. Inside the main defences, the enemy was occupying a well-fortified building which dominated the entire area around. At dawn on November 30, the attack was spearheaded by 'C' Company of 10 Mahar with its No. 9 platoon in the lead. Anusuya was part of the attacking platoon.

During the attack, the assaulting troops were held up by heavy automatic fire from enemy machine guns. It soon became apparent that the building would have to be neutralised before own troops could close in on the enemy bunkers surrounding it. Since it was not possible to call for air support or artillery fire due to the close proximity of own troops, it was decided to send a daredevil squad to get into the enemy defences by stealth and set the building on fire.

Sepoy Anusuya Prasad volunteered and taking a few phosphorous grenades, with utter disregard for his personal safety, crawled towards the enemy position. During the process, he was shot in both his legs but this gallant young soldier did not abandon his mission. He succeeded in crawling up to the building, selected it as his target and started crawling towards it. While doing so, he received a machine gun burst in his shoulders. Undeterred by his wounds and though bleeding profusely, he crawled up to the room with great difficulty and lobbed the grenades, setting the building on fire before succumbing to his wounds.

His gallant action forced the enemy to abandon the building. In this action, Sepoy Anusuya Prasad, in spite of his young age and inexperience, showed outstanding courage, with utter disregard to his personal safety and made the supreme sacrifice in the call of duty.

The moving picture of a very young Chitra Anusuya Prasad with Prime Minister Indira Gandhi is a reminder of the sacrifices made not only by the bravehearts, but also by their families. Two decades back, Chitra started an organization called Veer Shaheed Anusuya Prasad (MVC) Mahila Samiti in Dehradun, which works for women's empowerment. An inspirational couple—Sepoy Anusuya Prasad and Chitra Anusuya Prasad.

The Tribune

Lt Col Arun Bhimrao Harolikar

COMMISSIONED into the 3rd Battalion of the 5th Gorkha Infantry Regiment, Lt Col Arun Bhimrao Harolikar, from Kolhapur in Maharashtra, took over the command of 4/5 GR in 1971. The Maratha officer was with his men in all dangerous situations and also led the successful khukri charges on the war cry '*Jai Mahakali Aayo Gorkhali*'.

Displaying spectacular jointmanship, Harolikar heli-landed his battalion under fire at the gates of Sylhet, where his Gorkhas fought valiantly and successfully, preventing the enemy brigade from reinforcing Dhaka and coercing it sufficiently to surrender.

His conspicuous bravery earned him the Maha Vir Chakra. His citation reads:

On December 5, 1971, Lieutenant Colonel Arun Bhimrao Harolikar, who was commanding 4th Battalion of the 5th

Gorkha Rifles (4/5 GR), was given the task of capturing an enemy position in Eastern Theatre. When two assaulting companies were held up due to intense enemy fire, Lt Col Harolikar came forward and personally led the remaining two companies along the most difficult and unexpected approach from behind the enemy. On reaching the objective, on the battle cry '*Jai Mahakali— Aayo Gorkhali*', he personally led the charge and took part in hand-to-hand fighting, resulting in the capture of the enemy position.

On December 8, after landing of his battalion by helicopters behind Sylhet, the resolute fight by his Gorkhas under his inspiring leadership broke the enemy's will to resist, resulting in early surrender of the entire garrison of several thousand enemy personnel.

The Tribune

Rifleman Dil Bahadur Chhetri

IN hand-to-hand combat, Gorkhas are known to wield their shining khukri with effect. Rifleman Dil Bahadur Chhetri, after the MVC investiture ceremony, was asked whether he feared for his life when he came face to face with ten enemy soldiers during the 1971 war. His reply: 'A shining khukri in hand, and a Gorkha feels afraid? Have you ever heard of it?'

For the capture of the fortress-like Atgram defences in East Pakistan, for his single-handed dare-devilry, wiping out almost a section strength (ten men) of the enemy, Rifleman Chhetri was awarded the Maha Vir Chakra. The battle account reads:

> Rifleman Dil Bahadur Chhetri was part of 4/5 Gorkha Rifles battalion which was given the task of clearing the enemy position from Atgram. This was a well-fortified position and was held in strength by the enemy. During

the assault, the enemy brought down sustained and accurate fire from medium machine guns, inflicting heavy casualties on the Gorkhas. Rifleman Chhetri, realising the importance of silencing the machine gun, in complete disregard for his personal safety, drew his khukri and single-handedly charged at the bunker and killed eight enemy jawans who resisted his charge. He then caught the red-hot barrel of the machine gun, pulled it out and lobbed a grenade inside the bunker, killing the firing crew.

His determination and cool courage so inspired his comrades that they charged at the objective with great dash and captured it without any further casualties.

Second Lt Hawa Singh Chahal from Mirzapur village near Hisar (Haryana) and Rifleman Phas Bahadur Pun from Ramche village in Parbat district of Nepal also made the battalion proud by winning the Vir Chakras, posthumously.

Lance Havaldar Dil Bahadur Chhetri, MVC, quit the army voluntarily because of personal reasons even before completing the requisite pensionable service. He lived a very modest life in a remote Nepal village. His case was taken up when a senior officer of his unit got to know of his situation. Contact was established, and Rs 10 lakh was approved as a welfare measure to alleviate the hardships faced by the braveheart in his old age.

The Tribune

Lt Col Shamsher Singh, Second Lt Shamsher Singh Samra (Posthumous) and Lance Naik Ram Ugrah Pandey (Posthumous)

HOLLYWOOD producer Robert Evans, who produced *The Godfather*, has said that every story has three sides: your side, my side and the truth, and nobody is lying. At a 'stupid' border called Hilli on the eastern front, the three sides to the story here were Lt Col Shamsher Singh's, Second Lt Shamsher Singh Samra's and Lance Naik Ram Ugrah Pandey's.

Stories rich in truths also destroy shibboleths. Let's do it first up. The official line then, as now, is that the war began on

3 December 1971. That is a flat lie. What 8 Guards with the three MVCs were tasked to do is evidence that officialdom lies.

Lies mattered less than a line. A railway line, really, at a point where the border is so intricately carved that a little boy passing water in India could find it crossing an international boundary whichever way a gentle breeze blew. It is that stupid, the border 440 km north of Calcutta that Englishman Cyril Radcliffe had bequeathed to the sub-continent. The Partition of India was in reality the breaking up of two provinces—Punjab and Bengal—by squiggly lines.

Lt Col (later Maj. Gen.) Shamsher Singh was the Commanding Officer of 8th Battalion of the Brigade of the Guards. His battalion was chosen to attack the Pakistani position in Hilli—Hilli is on both sides of the border, the railway station being on the Pakistani side—on the night of 22–23 November, well before the formal announcement of hostilities. It was to be the 'bloodiest battle of the Bangladesh Liberation War', in the words of the Eastern Command chief, Lt Gen. Jagjit Singh Aurora. It was also the longest battle of attrition, lasting much longer than the Tangail airdrop of 11 December.

The Pakistani position was defended strongly. But therein lies another story, a Pakistani one, to be narrated later. Shamsher Singh's MVC citation reads:

> Lieutenant Colonel Shamsher Singh was commanding a battalion of the Brigade of Guards during an attack on a formidable position in the Eastern Sector. The enemy had put up formidable defences with well-coordinated artillery, tank and machine gun fire combined with mines, wire and booby traps. In spite of strong opposition from the enemy, the battalion launched a

series of counter-attacks during which the battalion ran short of ammunition. Undaunted, Lt Col Shamsher Singh engaged in hand-to-hand fighting. He personally directed his troops by moving from place to place and he encouraged his men to hold on to their positions and succeeded in capturing the objective, inflicting heavy casualties on the enemy.

That was only the beginning for 8 Guards. By the end of the war, the unit had fought five more battles. It had lost sixty-eight soldiers in the first battle itself. Hours before Shamsher Singh's soldiers launched the first attack on 22–23 November, the first air war had also taken place south-east from his position. Over Boyra, three Pakistani F-86 Sabres were shot down by Indian Gnats. One of the Pakistani pilots who ejected was rescued by a certain Capt. HS Panag, then adjutant for 4 Sikh. The pilot went on to become Pakistan's air chief decades later. (Panag, of course, is Lt Gen. Panag, who retired after heading India's northern and central commands). So much for the official line that the war began only on 3 December!

Up in Hilli, where 8 Guards had crossed the railway line, the Pakistanis put up a stiff fight. The 8 Guards were aiming at Morpara, north of the Pakistani defended position, which Lt Col Singh assigned to a Major to recce. One possibility would have been to use vehicles, but the terrain was boggy and swampy. Even the light PT-76 tanks would be grounded and become sitting ducks for the enemy. The Major was killed. But the position was critical. Shamsher Singh tasked his namesake, Shamsher Singh Samra, to take an RCL gun and head for it.

Second Lt (the rank does not exist in the Indian Army any longer) Shamsher Singh Samra was Platoon Commander with

'A' company. Along with his men, he was held back from the
destination by a machine gun nest. He pushed forward, despite
taking bullets on a shoulder. After overrunning the nest, they
came under fire from a flank. Shamsher Singh Samra's citation
reads:

> During the action, our troops came under heavy and
> accurate fire from automatic weapons. Undaunted by
> the heavy volume of fire, Second Lieutenant Shamsher
> Singh Samra encouraged his men to press home the
> attack. When the officer was about 25 yards from the
> position, he received a medium machine gun burst in
> the chest.

The twenty-five-year-old from Tarn Taran, schooled at DAV,
Shimla, died holding a grenade in his hand.

That was the nature of the battle of Hilli, where wave upon
wave of attacks was launched against entrenched and fortified
Pakistani positions. Hilli was not the real objective—that was
Bogra, a Brigade headquarters east of Hilli, not to be confused
with Boyra. The Indians wanted to intercept that to cut off the
Pakistan division headquarters at Natore with Rangpur in the
north.

Lance Naik Ram Ugrah Pandey was with a section that was
asked to try and bypass the entrenched Pakistani position in
Hilli. He was, says his citation,

> ... commanding a section of a company of a battalion of
> Brigade of Guards in an attack on an enemy post. The
> assaulting troops were held up by heavy and accurate
> fire from well-fortified enemy positions. Lance Naik

Pandey crawled up and destroyed in succession two enemy bunkers with hand grenades. He then took up a rocket launcher and destroyed a third bunker when he was mortally wounded and died on the spot.

Pandey (from Ghazipur in UP) was killed on 24 November 1971, also before the formal declaration of hostilities. His story did not die with him. It was kept alive for more than forty years by his widow, Shyama Devi, in Hema-Bansi village of Ghazipur district.

She kept fighting and pleading for a war widow's dues. She lived in a dilapidated house that leaked and was open to the elements. After running from pillar to post, she even wanted to return her husband's laurels. It was one more in a litany of stories of how memories of our soldiers can fade unless nurtured.

Even Shyama Devi's death—her requests for relief having been only partly met—is not the end of the twisty tale of the Battle of Hilli that saw three MVCs for a single Indian battalion, among other gallantry awards.

The defence of Hilli Bogra was commanded by Brig. (later Maj. Gen.) Tajammal Hussain Malik for Pakistan. 'The battle of Hilli Bogra sector in 1971 war can rightfully be regarded as a classic example of defence in the history of warfare,' he was to repeatedly say later. Malik refused to lay down arms even after 16 December, defying the orders of his shame-faced Eastern Commander, Lt Gen. AAK Niazi, who had signed the instrument of surrender in Dhaka. Indian troops had to drive his divisional commander to him from Natore two days later to make him hand over his service revolver.

Tajammal Malik's 205 Brigade was the only major one that the Indian Army could not break in East Pakistan. He admitted that his army had committed genocide and atrocities on the people of East Pakistan, and that this had made Bangladesh inevitable.

Nearly four decades after his release as a PoW and his promotion as a General, Malik died a bitter man, his thirst for revenge unquenched.

Frustration has sustained on both sides, despite the metal discs pinned to chests. That is the pity of stupid borders.

Sujan Dutta

Brig. Joginder Singh Bakshi, Brig. Antony Harold Edward Michigan, Lt Col Chittoor Venugopal and Havildar Bir Bahadur Pun

A squat tree bearing large jackfruit in the middle of the platform at a railway station called Darsana in Bangladesh became the butt of jokes in April 2008, when the Calcutta–Dhaka passenger train called Maitree Express was revived that month for the first time since Partition. Bengalis on both sides of the border joked that the fruit on one side of the tree is fatter than on the other. At Darsana, on the India–Bangladesh border, where the luxuriant jackfruit now fruits, there used to be a pillbox, with a machine gun barrel pointed towards India.

A grainy black-and-white photograph from newspapers of December 1971 shows five men in Indian Army uniform on the platform of the railway station, Darsana Halt. The standing man in the middle, capless, hands in his pockets, is Brig. Antony Harold Edward Michigan—Tony Michigan to his friends— Commander of 41 Mountain Brigade, which took Darsana from the Pakistan army in the Bangladesh war. Another officer in the picture is Lt Col Chittoor Venugopal, who commanded the 5/1 Gorkha Rifles. Both officers rose to the rank of Major General later in their careers.

These two, along with Brig. (later Lt Gen.) Joginder Singh Bakshi, who was commanding further north, and Havildar (later Honorary Captain) Bir Bahadur Pun, who served in Col Venugopal's battalion—all four Maha Vir Chakra awardees— illustrated what it took to wage battles in built-up (urban) areas in a country that was (and is) largely rural and full of water bodies.

In the areas along India's border with East Pakistan, rivers, streams, ponds and 'bils' (marshes) were natural obstacles. Across one such 'bil' from Balurghat in West Bengal's South Dinajpur district was a Pakistani post. The observer here reported to his senior one morning in December that the Indians were sending tanks towards him.

'You must be mistaken in the fog,' he was told over the radio. 'They must be buffaloes.'

'Except that,' said the observer, 'these buffaloes have 100 mm guns that are taking shots at my positions.'

It was pell-mell in the Pakistani ranks. Brig. Joginder Singh Bakshi (or 'Jogi') had sent a troop of PT-76 light tanks at the head of his infantry from 340 (Independent) Brigade for the first of a series of battles that was to conclude with the capture of the Pakistan brigade headquarters in Bogra, in the north-west sector of East Pakistan.

About a year before that, in 1970, Bakshi was leading operations against insurgents in Nagaland and Mizoram. 'You must learn from Jogi how to command a *paltan* in counter-insurgency operations,' Manekshaw had said at an infantry commanders' conference.

By December 1971, Bakshi had switched roles, and was now leading a brigade into urban warfare. His brigade, one of four in the 20 Infantry Division, was initially reserve. It was tasked to action first for Pirganj and later for Bogra after an attempted link-up failed because of stiff Pakistani resistance. This was the area where the Pakistan army refused to lay down arms on 16 December when Gen. AAK Niazi had signed the instrument of surrender.

'The 340 Brigade resumed advance to Pirganj and secured the north bank of the Karatoya (river) by December 10, but the southern bank was held by the enemy very strongly,' wrote KV Krishna Rao in his book, *Prepare or Perish: A Study of National Security*.

The 5/11 Gorkha Rifles that led the charge to Bogra 'poised itself behind enemy lines and turned its flank,' according to Lt Gen. JBS Yadava, who retired as Deputy Chief of Army Staff. The battalion was conferred the Battle Honour 'Bogra.' Brig. Bakshi's citation noted:

> Between December 7 and 16, 1971, the brigade under his (Bakshi's) leadership launched a series of successful attacks and captured a number of well-prepared enemy localities, culminating in the capture of Bogra, and by his daring execution outwitted the opposing forces

breaking their resistance and capturing a large number of men and equipment, including the commander of 205 Brigade of the Pakistan Army.

A few hundred kilometres south of Bakshi's position, the brigade led by Tony Michigan had a different task. It was already seeing action before the formal outbreak of hostilities on 3 December. By the end of November, Brig. Michigan had positioned his troops on the western periphery of the Jessore sector. Jessore was the second most important urban centre after Dhaka in the region of East Pakistan bordering West Bengal.

Michigan's objectives were Uthali and Darsana on the border and then a dash to Jhenaidah, 46 kms from Jessore. All of these, unlike the countryside, were fortified positions covered by Pakistani artillery and armour.

Michigan had been asked to capture Darsana by the last light of 4 December, a day after the formal declaration of war. After raids on Uthali, though, he had to regroup his forces. For this, he personally scouted the zone in the face of machine gun fire. Before that, the brigade had secured Pakistani border outposts.

Michigan's MVC citation reads:

Brigadier AHE Michigan was commanding a mountain brigade... In the attack on Uthali, a strongly fortified and heavily defended enemy position, when his troops were surrounded by enemy automatic and tank fire from three sides, he took personal control of the situation under heavy enemy fire. He conducted the battle with cool courage and disregard for his life and so inspired his troops that they took the objective by storm. Later, he launched the main offensive on Darsana and by sheer offensive spirit and personal example inspired his troops, who broke through a devastating hail of machine gun, artillery and mortar fire and gained a decisive victory.

In the area of responsibility of II Corps under Lt Gen. T Raina, there were two axes along which to advance. The divisional commander, Maj. Gen. MS Brar, opted for the shorter one, through Jibannagar–Kotchandpur–Kaliganj–Jhenaidah–Faridpur. This route was held up by Pakistani pillboxes and defences at Darsana.

Brig. Michigan tasked the 5/1 Gorkha Rifles battalion commanded by Lt Col Chittoor Venugopal to neutralize Darsana and crack through the defences. When Venugopal reached with his men, he found the town besieged by 22 Rajputs, but the Pakistan army was keeping them at bay.

Venugopal's MVC citation reads:

Lieutenant Colonel Chittoor Venugopal was commanding a battalion of Gorkha Rifles during the operations on the Eastern Front. On December 4, the battalion came up against well-fortified enemy defences at Uthali and Darsana. The position had a series of concrete pillboxes interconnected with elaborate communication trenches. Lt Col Venugopal planned the attack with great professional skill. Showing complete disregard for his personal safety, he led the attack and by his presence inspired his men to achieve the objective. After the capture of these two positions, the battalion relentlessly pursued the withdrawing enemy giving him no rest or time to regroup till Jhenaidah was captured three days later.

Lt Col Venugopal utilised the PT-76s, too, from 45 Cavalry. One of his rifle companies was assigned to capture the village of Chandpur, east of Darsana. Havildar Bir Bahadur Pun was in the company. It was laid low by heavy and medium machine gun fire from two sides. Before they knew it, some of his men were mowed down. Pun decided it was first important to track the trail of the fire.

Rolling into a nullah, he crawled up to a heavy machine gun nest, a pillbox dug into a mound surrounded by trees with sandbags around. He hurled two grenades into it. The gun was silenced; his men now took the position and went on to Jhenaidah. What they thought would be a dash took forty-eight hours, as the brigade had to traverse 50 kms. Pun's citation reads:

Havildar Bir Bahadur Pun was in a company of 1 GR, who were given the task of capturing village Chandpur, east of Darsana, on December 4, 1971. The assaulting troops came under heavy enemy artillery and small arms fire resulting in heavy casualties. On seeing a heavy machine gun post of the enemy, which was responsible for causing most of the casualties to his men, he rushed towards it through a nullah, crawled about 100 yards under heavy enemy fire, closed on to the bunker, lobbed two grenades and silenced the post. This act so inspired and motivated his men that the objective was taken within minutes.

Sujan Dutta

Brig. Vijay Kumar Berry, Maj. Vijay Rattan Chowdhary (Posthumous), Capt. Shankar Rao Walkar (Posthumous) and Capt. Pradip Kumar Gour (Posthumous)

ENDING a war is always a bloody mess. That was as true of the two-week hostilities between India and Pakistan fifty years ago as it is of the drawdown of the 'forever war' that the world witnessed in Afghanistan recently.

Even if India had a decisive surrender from the Pakistan Eastern Command in Dhaka on 16 December 1971 and an acceptance of a ceasefire on the western front on 17 December, there were bloody fights that took a heavy toll of lives beyond those dates, too.

Just as armed conflicts between India and Pakistan had broken out before the formal declaration of hostilities on 3 December, they continued after the formal cessation of the war, too. One of the bitterest in that order was in Rajasthan's Ganganagar sector. Nearly ten days after the ceasefire was accepted, Pakistan's army made an intrusion to set up a defended position atop two sand dunes over what was basically waste land of little or no strategic value. The firefights that followed came to be known as the 'Battle of the Sadiqia Sand Dunes' or the 'Battle of Nagi'.

Later chroniclers have pointed out that Pakistan's President Yahya Khan had described the fall of Dhaka and the signing of the instrument of surrender by his Eastern Command Chief Lt Gen. AAK Niazi as merely the loss of a battle, while the war would go on (reference: Major KC Praval's piece in the *Indian Defence Review*, 'Indian Army after Independence'). It was surmised that Pakistan wanted to claim a victory or stalemate in the west while its forces had collapsed in the east. Within twenty-four hours of that statement, better sense prevailed and Yahya Khan accepted the ceasefire.

At the Sadiqia dunes, however, Indian troops discovered on 25 December the incursion by a company of Pakistan's 36 Frontier Force and Rangers. It was supported by heavy artillery. They had also laid minefields to stop an Indian advance.

Maj. Vijay Kumar Berry, then leading Charlie Company of 4 Paras, was asked to secure the area. He was backed up by the 9 Para Field Regiment of artillery and the 410 Field Company of Engineers. Clearing the minefields while being subjected to shelling was done by the Engineers.

Just a week earlier, at Basantar, further north of Berry's position, Maj. Vijay Rattan Chowdhary of the 405 Field

Company of 9 Engineers Regiment had demonstrated what it takes to do this. His MVC citation reads:

> Major VR Chowdhary was in charge of minefield clearance of Chakra on the Western Front. The safe lanes had to be made with great speed to enable our tanks and anti-tank weapons to reach Chakra, which was in imminent danger of a counterattack by enemy armour. With utter disregard for his personal safety, Maj. Chowdhary personally supervised the operation, inspiring and motivating his men to their optimum efficiency. Throughout the advance, from December 5 onwards, Maj. Chowdhary displayed exemplary devotion to duty and was responsible for clearance of minefields of 1,000-1,500 yards depth at Thakurdwara, Lohra and Basantar river. While supervising the minefield lane near Basantar river, this gallant officer was killed due to enemy artillery fire. Maj. Chowdhary's exceptional devotion to duty, extraordinary bravery, inspiring leadership and supreme sacrifice was in the highest traditions of the Army.

Accounts of the battle in the desert describe how the dust and sand raised by the artillery had made visibility so difficult that the men could barely see who was leading. Pakistan's heavy guns took a heavy toll on the Indian Army. Maj. KC Praval (retd), a military analyst, estimated that 9 Para lost twenty-one men, including three officers, and had sixty wounded. Pakistan had employed more than seventy artillery pieces before the Indians re-took the position at great cost on 28 December.

Brig. Berry's citation reads:

After the ceasefire on December 17, 1971, Pakistani troops occupied an area of approximately 600 yards inside our territory in the Western Sector and developed this into a defended locality with minefields all around it. The locality was dominated by other defensive positions across the border held in strength by the enemy. A battalion of the Parachute Regiment was given the task of clearing this encroachment. Major Vijay Kumar Berry carried out the assault. Leading his men through the minefield, he charged the enemy position without any regard for his personal safety and captured the objective. The enemy, however, subjected the position to heavy artillery and mortar fire for the next twelve hours. Undaunted, Maj. Berry moved from section to section, inspiring his men and held on to the captured ground and cleared the intrusion.

An idea of what transpired in the battle is available from the experience of Capt. Shankar Rao Walkar. A mortar officer with 18 Madras, his detachment had advanced as much as about 70 km towards Hingore Tar. This was also on 16 December, when Niazi was surrendering his service revolver in Dhaka. Walkar was hit by splinters from shells, which tore him down as he ran between his mortar positions. His citation reads:

With utter disregard for his personal safety, Captain Walkar went to each company position to tie up defensive fire tasks. In doing so, he was hit twice by splinters and sustained injuries, but he refused to be evacuated and carried on with his task, displaying outstanding courage and devotion to duty. Heavy enemy shelling continued during the night and early next morning the enemy assaulted two company positions. Although wounded, Capt. Shankar Rao Shankhapan Walkar stuck to his job and brought very accurate mortar fire on the enemy and inflicted heavy casualties.

Capt. Walkar succumbed to his injuries.

Two days before that, as India and Pakistan played out a stalemate in the Chhamb and Shakargarh areas, Capt. Pradip Kumar Gour, who was an air observation officer providing vital intelligence on artillery and armour positions, was shot down by Pakistani Sabre jets. He was obstinate in continuing with his mission despite spotting danger. His citation reads:

Captain Pradip Kumar Gour was a pilot with an air observation post squadron deployed on the Western Front. Throughout the operations, he flew round-the-clock missions deep inside enemy territory, directing artillery fire and obtaining vital information about the enemy, undeterred by heavy small arms and artillery air burst fire. On December 14, 1971, while locating and registering targets deep inside enemy territory, Capt. Gour saw three enemy Sabre jets operating in the area. Instead of returning to the base and avoiding the danger, he decided to continue with the mission in view of its vital nature. He carried on with his mission evading the Sabre jets. Eventually, he was shot down.

In later remarks, General Andre Beaufre said that both sides on the western front had fought defensive battles. Also, the claims made by Pakistan did not match his own visual witnessing of the kind of damage it said it had inflicted on Indian troops. On the Indian side, he said, there was an unwillingness to push the advantage and take the battle to the enemy territory. But that conclusion does not necessarily mean the Indians were wrong. It was part of their operational plan to go for the jugular in the east while holding ground in the west. Even that was terribly costly for India, as the battle of the sand dunes shows.

Sujan Dutta

Lt Gen. Joginder Singh Gharaya, Lt Col Surinder Kapur, Maj. Anup Singh Gahlaut (Posthumous) and Naik Sugan Singh (Posthumous)

T HE 'Pippas' lurched through the bush and swamp, crossed a rickety bridge with half of their tracks sticking out, and 'felt' their way ahead with a crewman sitting on the hull and lighting the way ahead with a torch. In the narrow channel within which they had to follow their course, a step out could mean getting bogged down or being blown up by an anti-tank mine. A mine, in fact, ripped the bottom out of one.

'Pippa' was what the men of 45 Cavalry called the PT-76 tank. The Russian name for it was Plavayushchiy Tank, or floating tank, but the Indian soldiers were using the word to describe a tin can floating on water. The Pippa was indispensable to the Indian forces in south-western East Pakistan (now Bangladesh), who liberated the first district, Jessore, on 6 December.

Infantry troops piggybacked on, or floated behind and followed the Pippas through a heavily defended Burinda, where Pakistan's 107 Brigade put up a stiff defence. But before Burinda fell, the brigade held back an offensive by 1 Jammu and Kashmir Rifles commanded by Lt Col Surinder Kapur. Kapur and his men were in danger of being overrun, but for three days, they fought on as the Pakistani brigade headquarters at Jessore, to its east, decamped and made for Khulna to the south.

East Pakistan (Bangladesh) was a watery landscape, with Bengali villages that typically had ponds with 'bundhs', or embankments, around them. These were reinforced by the Pakistani brigade with concrete bunkers, which slowed down the Indian march to Jessore from the west to the east. Lt Col Surinder Kapur's citation reads:

> Lieutenant Colonel Surinder Kapur was commanding a battalion of the J&K Rifles on the Eastern Front. His battalion was given the task of taking up a defensive position in the Jessore sector to blunt enemy attacks and inflict maximum casualties on him. Lt Col Kapur displayed great professional acumen and leadership in deploying his battalion in spite of being under enemy artillery and small arms fire. The enemy launched five attacks, in strength, on his battalion position in three days. On each occasion, Lt Col Kapur, showing utter disregard for his personal safety, moved from one locality to another exhorting his men to stand fast. Inspired by his presence and cool courage, his battalion repulsed all enemy attacks, inflicting heavy casualties.

Burinda was finally taken by 4 Sikh with the help of the squadron of Pippas. Lt Gen. HS Panag, who was then an adjutant with the battalion, has detailed the fall of Burinda ('Army first beat the Pakistanis in their minds, battle of Burinda is one example', *The Print*), which Brig. BS Mehta, who had earlier taken command of a squadron in the middle of a tank-to-tank war, has called 'The Burinda Bash'. Burinda took much longer to fall than Jessore.

Mehta's account, part of a compilation of experiences of the war by graduates of the 1966 batch from the IMA, shows that the 'bash' was often agonizingly slow.

Mehta was standing atop his tank when 'one savage sweepback of the cupola hinge resulted in hitting my nose and knocked off a few teeth'.

The battles leading to the fall of Jessore and Khulna were fought by three infantry brigades: 42, 350 and 32 (going from north to south). Jessore itself fell practically without any bloodshed.

Brig. (later Lt Gen.) Joginder Singh Gharaya was commanding 42 Brigade. He was hit by shrapnel from Pakistani artillery. He continued, having had the experience of being wounded in battle earlier, too. He was attacked during the Hyderabad Police action in September 1948. His citation reads:

Brigadier JS Gharaya was commanding an infantry brigade in the Jessore sector on December 6, 1971. His brigade was attacked on four successive occasions and despite heavy casualties, his troops stood the ground due largely to his excellent tactical handling, outstanding courage, constant presence and guidance.

His conduct of this operation was responsible for heavy enemy losses and their withdrawal. During the

subsequent offensive operations, Brig. Gharaya was
with the leading troops when he was severely wounded
by enemy fire. He refused to be evacuated till he had
seen the attack through as the success of this attack was
vital to our further advance in Bangladesh.

There was not much bloodshed in Jessore, Sydney Schanberg
reported for *The New York Times*. That was because the
Pakistani forces had experienced a mutiny in their ranks
and were deeply unpopular. The Mukti Joddha's leader, Maj.
Manjoor, was in contact with the Indian forces through the
battles.

The battles within East Pakistan were contrasting, even
though they were contained within a single geographical unit.
This was not only a consequence of the variations in terrain
and topography, but also an outcome of the nature of defences
that Lt Gen. AAK Niazi had planned, with spaced-out fortified
structures, many of which the Indian troops bypassed to finally
reach Dhaka.

While in south-west East Pakistan there were battles that
went on for days, in the east and south-east, before Lt Gen. Sagat
Singh's dramatic Meghna airlift, there were smaller attempts to
get behind enemy lines and/or establish roadblocks. This was
the case in Brig. Tom Pande's 61 Mountain Brigade area.

Maj. Anup Singh Gahlaut's 3 Dogras in the area were tasked
with putting up roadblocks behind enemy lines between
Lakshan and Chauddagram to the east and north of the
important town of Comilla. Gahlaut's citation reads:

He infiltrated his company through enemy lines,
established a roadblock and inflicted heavy casualties

on the enemy. Subsequently, a company of his battalion came under heavy enemy pressure and Major Gahlaut volunteered to go to the assistance of the company. In this mission, he led a platoon and successfully pinned down the enemy company by bringing effective small arms fire on them. His position was, however, attacked by the enemy from a different direction. Undeterred by the overwhelming superiority of the enemy, he rallied his men and succeeded in breaking the enemy attack. Having been mortally wounded in hand-to-hand fighting, he died shortly after his heroic battle.

The 7th battalion of the Rajputana Rifles was given a comparable mission in the low hills of Mynamati. Naik Sugan Singh was commanding an assaulting section. An earlier air raid by Indian MiG-21s had been partially successful, knocking out a Pakistani tank but unable to take down the defences. The battalion was ordered to attack the reinforced concrete bunkers that housed medium machine gun nests.

Naik Sugan Singh's MVC citation reads:

When the assaulting troops closed in on the objective, two medium machine guns opened fire and held up the assault. Naik Sugan Singh charged at one of them. He received a burst in his shoulder. Although bleeding profusely, he crawled up to the bunker and lobbed a hand grenade, killing two men. Although he had bled profusely, he charged at the second medium machine gun; he could not carry himself far and fell down. But undeterred, he pushed a grenade into the bunker, killing three of the enemy. He himself was also killed.

Sujan Dutta

Lt Col Ved Prakash Ghai
(Posthumous)

FROM the battles fought on the western front between Degh Nadi and Bein river emerged two PVC awardees (Maj. Hoshiar Singh and Second Lt Arun Khetarpal) and eight Maha Virs, including Lt Col VP Ghai.

An alumnus of DAV College, Dehradun, Lt Col Ved Prakash Ghai led 16 Madras from the front as they blunted three counter-attacks to dislodge his battalion from the bridgehead established by it. He was killed in action, but not before ensuring that his gallant Thambis held on to the bridgehead that they had established at a heavy cost.

Lt Col Ghai was awarded the Maha Vir Chakra for outstanding command of his battalion. The battle account reads:

At 1930 hours on December 15, during phase 1 of the Division attack, Lieutenant Colonel Ved Prakash Ghai, commanding 16 Madras, led his battalion for the capture of Lalial and Sarajchak as a part of the bridgehead operation. The positions were captured after some of the sharpest hand-to-hand encounters. The enemy launched many counter-attacks at night to dislodge the battalion but under the inspiring leadership of Lt Col Ghai, his men beat back all attacks.

As the day dawned, the enemy again launched a determined counter-attack supported by artillery and armour. With utter disregard to personal safety, Lt Col Ghai moved fearlessly from one company position to another, encouraging his men. Inspired by his fearlessness, bravery and leadership, the battalion repulsed the attacks with heavy losses to the enemy. However, a stray bullet by the withdrawing enemy caught him in the chest, wounding him seriously. Before he could be evacuated, Lt Col Ghai died on the battlefield but not before ensuring that his battalion held on to the bridgehead for three nights and two days steadfastly against all possible odds.

The Tribune

Lt Col Ved Prakash Airy

A N alumnus of Government School, Karnal, Lt Col
Ved Prakash Airy took over the command of the 3rd
Grenadiers in April 1971. In the morning hours of 5 December,
the battalion, as part of 47 Infantry Brigade, was ordered to
cross the International Border and 'Bash on Regardless' (the
motto of 54 Infantry Division).

On the night of 5/6 December, 3rd Grenadiers crossed
the border. The first interference came at Bhaironath, but the
bold planning by Lt Col Airy ensured that by the first light on
6 December, the defended locality was captured, along with
three prisoners of war and two Sherman tanks.

For the main task, the 3rd Grenadiers spearheaded Phase 2
of the 54 Infantry Division attack and, under the leadership of
Lt Col Airy, earned the title 'PVC Battalion' by capturing the
heavily defended Jarpal deep inside Pakistan.

Lt Col Airy was awarded the Maha Vir Chakra. The battle account reads:

> The 3rd Grenadiers was tasked to capture heavily defended localities of Jarpal and Lohal on the night of December 15/16, with a view to establish a bridgehead on Basantar Nadi for the tanks to break out. Lt Col Airy led his troops fearlessly even when his men were fighting the enemy hand-to-hand. Though the casualties of the battalion were marginally high, both objectives were captured. But after regrouping, the enemy counter-attacked in the morning hours on December 16, followed by the attacks supported by the tanks to dislodge the Grenadiers from the bridgehead but all the counter-attacks were ruthlessly beaten back one after the other.
>
> During the battle, unmindful of his personal safety, Lt Col Airy moved from one Company to the other, with just his cap balaclava as headgear, motivating his men to hold the captured ground. Noticing the firm resolve of the Grenadiers, the enemy finally retreated with heavy losses.

To his credit, Lt Col Airy, before endorsing the bravery of his battalion's officers and men, did the honour to the bravehearts of the supporting arms, including Second Lt Arun Khetarpal of The Poona Horse, Capt. Satish Sehgal of 75 Medium Regiment, Maj. Prahalad Toro of 161 Field Regiment and Capt. RN Gupta of 9 Engineer Regiment.

He also displayed a high level of professionalism by recommending his counterpart, Lt Col Mohd Akram Raja,

Commanding Officer of 35 Frontier Forces of the Pakistan army, whose body was recovered with bullet marks on the forehead and the right hand firmly gripping his sten gun, for the highest gallantry decoration in Pakistan. Lt Col Raja was awarded 'Hilal-i- Jur'at', the second highest gallantry decoration in Pakistan.

The Tribune

Havildar Thomas Phillipose

BELONGING to Kerala, Havildar Thomas Phillipose of 16 Madras etched his name as a Maha Vir in the Battle of Basantar (western front) during the 1971 war. The 1942-born Havildar Phillipose, who retired as an Honorary Captain, was awarded the Maha Vir Chakra for courage and gallantry in the face of immense odds.

Phillipose's MVC citation reads:

Havildar T. Phillipose was a platoon commander in a battalion of the Madras Regiment during the Battle of Basantar on the night of 15 December 1971. Casualties in the platoon were heavy and when the objective was captured, the enemy counterattacked. Havildar Phillipose led a brave counter-charge with fixed bayonets with his meagre strength. He enthused and inspired this small force with his leadership and bravery. Although he received a severe bullet wound himself, the charge led by him was so determined and brave that the enemy got demoralised and fled.

Throughout, Havildar Phillipose displayed resolute leadership under adverse conditions and set a brilliant example of courage and devotion to duty in keeping with the highest traditions of the Army.

Major PV Sahadevan and Naik Sahadevan of 16 Madras, too, performed beyond the call of duty and earned Vir Chakras.

The Tribune

Lt Col Hanut Singh

KNOWN as the 'Saint Soldier', the tall and lean Lt Gen. Hanut Singh achieved legendary status in the armed forces. He was an extraordinary officer—bold, fearless, a thorough professional, and a mentor like few others.

He was from Jasol near Barmer in Rajasthan, and came from a family of cavalry officers. He was commissioned into The Poona Horse on 4 December 1952. There is no dearth of stories surrounding the persona and achievements of Hanut Singh, but the Maha Vir Chakra bestowed on him for his exploits in the 1971 war would rank high on the list.

As Commanding Officer (Commandant in Armoured Corps) of 17 Horse, Lt Col Hanut Singh was tasked with establishing a bridgehead across Basantar Nadi in the Shakargarh sector. Leading from the front across the heavily mined dry riverbed, he successfully defended the bridgehead before the infantry advanced. And despite repeated attacks supported by the armour, the Pakistanis failed to push back the Indian infantry or dislodge The Poona Horse from the bridgehead. The Indian tank crews took a heavy toll on the Patton tanks, forcing the enemy to retreat. The Poona Horse won one PVC, two MVCs and four VrCs in the battle.

Lt Col Hanut Singh's Maha Vir Chakra citation reads:

> Lieutenant Colonel Hanut Singh was commanding 17 Horse in Shakargarh sector. On December 16, his regiment was inducted into the Basantar river bridgehead and took up positions ahead of the infantry. The enemy launched a number of armoured attacks in strength on December 16 and 17. Undeterred by the enemy medium artillery and tank fire, Lt Col Hanut Singh moved from one threatened sector to another with total disregard to personal safety. His presence and cool courage inspired his men to remain steadfast and perform commendable acts of bravery.

There were no safe lanes for the tanks to cross over, even though the Engineers had frantically cleared the mines. Bold as ever, Lt Col Hanut Singh directed his squadrons to head for the bridgehead, with himself in the lead in his command tank.

Fortune favours the brave, and he ranked among the bravest. Not a single anti-tank mine came in his way while he crossed the river bed. The legend of Hanut Singh only got fortified.

The Tribune

Maj. Amarjit Singh Bal

AN alumnus of Lawrence School, Sanawar, like Second Lt Arun Khetarpal, PVC, and from the same regiment, The Poona Horse, Major Amarjit Singh Bal, too, etched his name in the highest portals of valour during the Battle of Basantar.

As Maj. Hoshiar Singh of the 3rd Grenadiers was organizing defences after the capture of the strategically important Jarpal, the Pakistan army's 35 Frontier Force battalion, supported by armour, launched a full-blown counter-attack. However, before the enemy could reach within assaulting distance, Maj. Bal, with his B Squadron, reached and deployed tanks on the right flank of the Grenadiers. On the left flank was Second Lt Khetarpal.

The Grenadiers held the ground as Maj. Bal took the enemy armour twice in strength head-on and inflicted a heavy toll on the enemy Patton tanks. For the short yet intense battle,

Maj. Bal was awarded the Maha Vir Chakra. The excerpts from the battle account read:

> Major Amarjit Singh Bal was commanding Bravo Squadron of 17 Horse during the Battle of Basantar. On the morning hours of December 16, the enemy launched a number of determined counter-attacks supported by tanks to re-capture Jarpal, which had been captured by the 3rd Grenadiers after suffering unimaginable casualties. Though heavily outnumbered, Major Bal displayed exemplary courage, determination and aggressive spirit and by his personal example motivated his squadron to remain steadfast and resolute. He, along with his squadron tank crews, did not let even a single Patton tank reach Jarpal village, steadfastly held by the 'Charlie' Company of 3rd Grenadiers under the command of Major Hoshiar Singh. Under the bold and aggressive leadership of Major Bal, his squadron repulsed all armour counter-attacks with heavy losses to the enemy.

The Indian Centurion tanks took on the superior Patton tanks of Pakistan and proved that more than the weapon, it is the man behind it and his training that determine the outcome.

The Tribune

Lt Col Raj Mohan Vohra

LT Gen. Raj Mohan Vohra passed out from the IMA along with Lt Gen. Hanut Singh in the same year, 1952. And, like Hanut Singh, he, too, won the Maha Vir Chakra during the 1971 war.

A product of St Edward's School, Shimla, Raj Mohan, like all three of his brothers, joined the Army. He was commissioned into 14 Horse (Scinde Horse) and, rising up the ranks, was given the command of 4 Horse (Hodson's Horse) during the 1971 war. 4 Horse was raised as Hodson's Horse by Captain William Hodson. During the First War of Independence, Hodson captured Bahadur Shah Zafar, had him transported to Burma and killed his two sons. After Independence, there was a clamour for a name change. The 4 Horse has a formidable combination of one Dogra and two Sikh squadrons.

For his inspiring leadership and personal gallantry during the 1971 war in the western sector, Lt Col Raj Mohan Vohra was awarded the Maha Vir Chakra. His citation reads:

Lieutenant Colonel Raj Mohan Vohra was commanding 4 Horse in Shakargarh sector. His regiment spearheaded the advance capturing Bhairo Nath, Thakurdwara, Bari Lagwal, Chakra and Dehlra. Each of these positions was fortified with tanks, missiles and minefields. With complete disregard to personal safety, Lt Col Vohra moved well forward inspiring his squadrons. Lt Col Vohra, the Commandant, standing on the turret of his tank, often along with the frontline tank crews, greatly enthused his officers and men. Inspired by his personal example and courage, his regiment stood fast against repeated attacks by the enemy armour and destroyed 27 enemy tanks, the highest count during the entire war, with minimal losses to his regiment.

The list of braves was long; all the three Squadron Commanders of 4 Horse—Majors Suraj Jit Chaudhary, Govind Singh and Kamal Nanda—were awarded the Vir Chakra.

The Tribune

Lt Col RK Singh

COMMISSIONED into 13 Punjab (Jind Infantry), an erstwhile Jind State Force battalion which got amalgamated with the Indian Army, Lt Col RK Singh assumed the command of 14 Punjab (Nabha Akal) in 1971.

Thirteen days before the declaration of war, the Pakistan army launched a massive attack near Garibpur village, 7 km inside south-western East Pakistan, on 21 November. The Battle of Garibpur is a shining example of textbook synergy between the Indian Army's combat arms. The armour took on the enemy armour in equal number head-on and nearly decimated the latter, the artillery left no stone unturned in assisting the infantry beat back repeated attacks, and the Engineers (just about 30 Sappers) excelled in their infantry role, too. But it was the infantry that held the ground steadfastly.

The 6th and 21st Punjab battalions of Pakistan's 107 Infantry Brigade, supported by the 49th and 55th Field Regiments (artillery) and 3 Independent Armoured Squadron (Chaffees), attacked Nabha Akal as it was setting up defences in the Jessore sector.

Keeping a cool head, Lt Col Singh kept his faith in the Nabha Akals and the supporting combat arms—the Gunners, the tankmen and the Sappers—as they foiled the formidable attack in the four-hour battle.

For his role during the Battle of Garibpur, Lt Col RK Singh was awarded the Maha Vir Chakra. His citation reads:

> Lt Col Raj Kumar Singh, who was commanding a battalion of the Punjab Regiment, was assigned the task of occupying a defended area between villages Garibpur–Jagannathpur on the eastern front to contain the enemy intruding into Indian territory. He planned and organised the defences held by his battalion with great skill and professional competence.
>
> The enemy attacked the battalion defended area with two infantry battalions and a squadron of tanks. Lt Col Singh directed his troops with great courage and confidence. With utter disregard for his personal safety, he moved from one company locality to another, inspiring his junior commanders and troops. The enemy launched three determined attacks but all were beaten back with heavy losses. Throughout, Lt Col Raj Kumar Singh displayed exemplary courage, outstanding leadership and personal gallantry.

Three enemy Sabres were also shot down by three Indian Gnats in a dogfight. Prime Minister Indira Gandhi broke the tradition by mentioning this battle in Parliament on 24 November, giving details of the tanks and aircrafts destroyed when the war had not yet been declared.

The Tribune

Maj. DS Narang (Posthumous)

'CHIEFY', as he was popularly known, Maj. Daljit Singh Narang was commissioned into the Deccan Horse in 1956 and joined the newly raised 45 Cavalry Regiment in 1965. He was in command of 'C' Squadron of 45 Cavalry in support of 42 Infantry Brigade ex 9 Infantry Division. On 21 November, he was destined to play a decisive role in beating back the biggest enemy attack of the 1971 war in East Pakistan.

For his exemplary leadership and outstanding personal gallantry during the tank-versus-tank battle (the only one in the eastern theatre), Maj. Daljit Singh 'Chiefy' Narang was awarded the MVC, posthumously. The account of his conspicuous bravery reads:

> During Operation 'Cactus Lily', Major Daljit Singh Narang was commanding a squadron of a cavalry

regiment in support of an infantry battalion which was attacked by two enemy battalions supported by a squadron of Chaffee tanks. He skilfully and boldly manoeuvred his squadron despite heavy enemy fire and personally knocked out one enemy tank from the closest range. With utter disregard for his personal safety and undeterred by the enemy tank and anti-tank weapons fire, he directed the fire of his squadron standing on the turret of his tank.

His courage and fearlessness so inspired his command that they successfully decimated the enemy squadron of Chaffee tanks and stemmed the enemy advance. Major Narang, however, was killed atop his tank by enemy machine gun fire while leading his squadron.

Throughout this action, the conspicuous bravery, devotion to duty and supreme sacrifice of Major Narang were in the highest traditions of the Indian Army.

Assuming command in the trying circumstances, Capt. Balram Singh Mehta, the Squadron Second-in-Command, took off from where the braveheart 'Chiefy', Maj. Narang, had left. The squadron left Garibpur littered with the carcasses of Pakistani Chaffee tanks.

The Tribune

Subedar Malkiat Singh
(Posthumous)

SUBEDAR Malkiat Singh was enrolled in 14 Punjab (Nabha Akal) in 1951. For his conspicuous bravery, he was awarded the Maha Vir Chakra, posthumously. His citation reads:

Subedar Malkiat Singh was platoon commander of No. 9 Platoon of 'C' Company of 14 Punjab (Nabha Akal), which was occupying a defended area around villages Garibpur and Jagannathpur. On November 21, his platoon was attacked by the enemy in overwhelming strength. Subedar Malkiat, undeterred, crawled from trench to trench encouraging his men to hold fast. He told all his section commanders to open fire only on his orders. He let the enemy come as close as 50 yards and then ordered fire. The entire platoon opened up with all platoon weapons, including lobbing of grenades. However, despite devastating fire, a section of Punjabis from Pakistan's 6th Punjab battalion rushed closer than 50 yards and bravely fought the Punjabis of Indian 14th Punjab. In half an hour, hand-to-hand fight ensued; Pakistani Punjabis took a heavy toll on Malkiat's platoon, but withdrew after having been overpowered by the Indian Punjabis. Subedar Malkiat remained in the thick of the close-quarter battle till he was fatally bayoneted.

Twenty gallantry awards were won in the Battle of Garibpur—three MVCs and seven Vir Chakras (three to top guns of the IAF).

As a PoW, Brig. Hayat Khan, Commander of Pakistan's 107 Infantry Brigade, said:

As a result of this battle, not just my brigade but our entire 9th Infantry Division got completely unbalanced. The path to Jessore lay open and my brigade had no tanks left to support it in its future operations. Your PTs were no match to my Chaffees but I suppose that day the luck was on your side.

The Tribune

Lt Col KL Rattan

TWO memorable defensive battles were fought south of Banihal Pass, amidst the rigours of the Pir Panjal mountains of Poonch and the undulating rough plains of Chhamb-Jaurian, west of Munnawar Tawi. The assaulting enemy numbered several times the Indian soldiers who manned the defences; however, they were met squarely with rare steadfastness, valour and dedication, and crushing defeats were inflicted on the enemy in both these encounters.

The 6 Sikh ('Chhe', as popularly known) occupied defences over a 13-km frontage on the heights above Poonch; two of these, Points 405 and 406, were of strategic importance, standing as sentinels. Loss of these would directly threaten Poonch town itself. Pakistan had always prized these options, and on the night intervening 3 and 4 December, it launched a heavy punch at both points with two brigades (six battalions). Coincidently, one of these was the 5th Frontier Force, originally the 53 Royal Sikhs! Two enemy battalions launched feint attacks, while one infiltrated to cut off the road leading to Poonch. 'Chhe', fully entrenched, lay in their path to upset the enemy's well-laid-out plans.

The artillery bombardment announced the enemy's intent; an advance position at the helipad, held by two platoons under Capt. Mamik, received the heavy rush, but they stood rock solid. A young Sepoy, Sampuran Singh, manning a light machine gun (LMG) stood out. His citation states: 'He poured ceaseless rapid fire on the incoming enemy; a head injury didn't perturb him, he stuck to his assigned task till he was unconscious due to loss of blood and was only then evacuated.' Repeated attacks were beaten back, and the heavy casualties inflicted held up the attack. These troops achieved their task of delaying the enemy and, as planned, pulled back to the defences on Point 405.

Soon, the next position at 'Tund' was under bi-directional attack. Maj. Punjab Singh, the company commander, 'was the man of the moment; he quickly readjusted the defences and beat back the enemy on the first night. The next night, when the enemy returned, Punjab Singh had skilfully positioned the reinforcements and rushed forward.' Two junior leaders, Havildar Malkiat Singh and Naib Singh, need special mention. With disregard for their own safety, they struck the enemy where most wanted. The enemy withdrew, their bodies and weapons scattered all over. Desperate, the enemy sent in their Special Service Group (SSG), which managed to come within 30–40 metres of Point 405, but was also forced back.

From 3 December till the dawn of 7 December, the true mettle of Lt Col (later Maj Gen.) KL Rattan was on full display— 'unmindful of the heavy shelling and firing, he was present wherever an attack developed; with his skillful professionalism, he ensured the right moves, his hearty words kept the men in high morale and charged up throughout', says the citation. He was awarded the Maha Vir Chakra. His motivational attitude energized Sepoy Safaiwala Mangat Ram, 'who without any fear or adversity continuously supplied ammunition to points under attack till his last breath, and was killed in the act'.

Five Vir Chakras were awarded in this fight—to Maj. Punjab Singh, Havildar Malkiat Singh, Sepoy Sampuran Singh, Naik Naib Singh and Sepoy Safaiwala Mangat Ram (the latter two were posthumously awarded).

The defence of Poonch has gone down as one of the most successful defensive actions by any battalion in India; the defenders were deservedly awarded the Battle Honour 'Defence of Poonch' and the Theatre Honour 'Jammu and Kashmir'. After the war, special appreciation of outstanding valour displayed by an enemy soldier, identified as Lance Naik Noor Shahjahan, was conveyed to the enemy, which led to his being awarded the 'Sitar-e-Jurat', the third highest Pakistani award for gallantry.

Lt Gen. Raj Sujlana (Retd)

Lt Col Prem Kumar Khanna and
Maj. Jaivir Singh

THE Chhamb-Jaurian sector, west of Jammu and bulging towards Pakistan, is, in military terms, considered a 'soft belly' of the defences, as Pakistan has a tremendous advantage here, which it has repeatedly exploited. 1971 was no different, as Pakistan launched its major offensive here, aiming to capture Akhnoor and cut off the main Rajouri–Poonch axis. Pakistan employed its 23rd Infantry Division with five infantry brigades (fifteen battalions), three armoured regiments (approximately 150 tanks) and paramilitary forces. The 5 Sikh went on to fight an epic defensive battle here.

Earthquake-like, the ground shook on and around the Indian forward posts at around 2100 hours on 3 December as Pakistani artillery opened its barrage. The initial targets were our posts at Pir Jamal and Moel, and by midnight, the posts at Phagla, Mandiala and Point 303. These posts and Point 303 were under the command of Maj. DS Pannu, an intrepid soldier and an outstanding sportsman with a special passion for riding. Like a true, aggressive horseman, not caring for personal safety, he rushed to join his forward troops at Pir Jamal and Moel, which were soon under intense attack by tanks and infantry. The small Indian force beat back three attacks, which delayed the enemy for sixteen hours and upset their overall plan.

The casualties were heavy, but Maj. Pannu, with a handful of survivors, pulled back to his main position at Point 303, which, too, soon came under attack. The enemy was held up through 4 December, and on the evening of 5 December, Maj. Pannu was killed. Point 303 fell for a short time, but the gallant Capt. Kamal Bakshi rose to the occasion and counter-attacked. The post was regained, but Capt. Bakshi went missing in action, reportedly killed. The surroundings were strewn with the bodies of enemy soldiers; two medium machine guns (MMGs) and seventy rifles were recovered from the enemy.

Simultaneously, Phagla, some distance away, also came under heavy attack. The company was led by the dynamic Maj. Jaivir Singh, who was at the forefront. The battle raged for seventy-two hours; repeated attacks were beaten back. The enemy managed penetration at one point, but 'Maj Jaivir Singh led a counter-attack, stiff hand-to-hand fighting followed, the enemy withdrew. If this was not enough, a nearby post overrun by the enemy was counter-attacked and regained.' The officers and troops were near exhaustion, but the inspiring leadership of Lt Col Prem Khanna, 'whose cool, calculated courage, skill and imaginative tactics ensured that incessant attacks by overwhelming numbers of infantry and armour were beaten back, his directions and personal touch ensured a high level of will of his men!'

The 5 Sikh lost two officers, a JCO and thirty-nine other ranks, but the enemy paid with 586 killed and a costly lesson in battling the Sikh troops. The *Defence Journal* of Pakistan, in one of its issues, acknowledged 'the tenacious courage of 5 Sikh and troops of 9 Deccan Horse' and remarked, 'If the Indian commander now knows full details of what was coming for him on the morning of December 5, he can rightly congratulate the CO of 5 Sikh and the tank troop commander ... they saved a sad day for him!'

The 5 Sikh was decorated with the Theatre Honour 'Jammu & Kashmir', Lt Col Prem Khanna and Maj. Jaivir Singh with the Maha Vir Chakra, and Maj. DS Pannu and Naik Richhpal Singh with the Vir Chakra. Capt. Bakshi was mentioned in dispatches.

Lt Gen. Raj Sujlana (Retd)

Brig. Mohinder Lal Whig

FOR his bold planning, and quite often for being in the forefront to ensure execution of his plans, Brig. Mohinder Lal Whig, ex Gorkha Rifles, from the reputed Whig family of Amritsar, was awarded the Maha Vir Chakra for commanding 121 Independent Infantry Brigade during the 1971 war.

His MVC citation reads:

Brigadier Mohinder Lal Whig was the commander of an infantry brigade group in the Kargil sector on the Westem Front. His Brigade was assigned the task of capturing the complex of enemy posts overlooking Kargil and to advance to 'Olthing Thang'. These pickets located on dominating heights were well fortified and protected with wire obstacles and mines. Brigadier Mohinder Lal Whig planned the operation with professional competence and skill. In spite of the altitude being over 12,000 feet and the temperature 20 degrees below zero, he led his troops with determination and by his presence and cool courage inspired his men to brave the enemy shelling and small arm fire and capture 36 enemy posts within a short period of 10 days, inflicting heavy losses on the enemy and capturing large quantities of arms and ammunition.

During this operation, Brigadier Mohinder Lal Whig displayed conspicuous gallantry and outstanding leadership in keeping with the highest traditions of the Army.

The Tribune

Col Udai Singh

COLONEL Udai Singh, a Rathore Rajput from Gharaha village in Jodhpur, was commissioned into the 8th Gorkha Rifles in 1950. In 1971, he was given the command of three Ladakh Scouts infantry companies and a section each of mortars and machine guns to recapture Indian territory from Chalunka to Turtuk north of Leh, held strongly by a PoK infantry battalion in Nubra.

It was due to the sheer determination of Col Udai and his Gorkhas fighting against all possible odds that today, not just Tyakshi, Turtuk and Chalunka, but also around 800 sq. km of territory is back with India.

For his conspicuous gallantry, outstanding leadership and cool courage in the face of the enemy, Col Udai Singh was awarded the Maha Vir Chakra. His citation reads:

Colonel Udai Singh was in charge of a force consisting of three companies of the Ladakh Scouts and a section each of mortars and medium machine guns, which had been assigned the task of capturing the area from Chalunka to Turtuk in the Kargil sector. The task involved movement on man pack and animal transport mostly by night in sub-zero temperatures at an altitude up to 18,000 feet through unreconnoitered area. Colonel Udai Singh completely outmanoeuvred the enemy, followed him and pressed home the attack against well-entrenched positions.

Throughout this period, Colonel Udai Singh was in the forefront sharing the discomfort and danger with his troops. By his presence and cool courage, he inspired his force to attack and capture a series of formidable posts after bitter fighting and often at the point of bayonet. Throughout the 10-day operations, Colonel Udai Singh displayed conspicuous gallantry, outstanding leadership, cool courage in the face of the enemy and also professional skill of a high order in keeping with the highest traditions of the Army.

The Tribune

Subedar Mohinder Singh

SUBEDAR Mohinder Singh, who was from Sham Nagar village in Amritsar district, was commanding No. 9 platoon of 'C' Company, a Sikh company of 18 Punjab, in the Kargil sector during the 1971 war, when he went way beyond the call of duty. He led his platoon uphill from the front for the capture of a height that had defied capture by the Indian Army's earlier attempts twice over. He was undeterred by this earlier record.

After reaching the assaulting distance, he gave the cry '*Bole So Nihal*', and the mighty Sikhs of No. 9 platoon of 18 Punjab bayoneted one enemy after the other, with Subedar Mohinder in the lead. After half an hour of hand-to-hand fighting, the highest point that overlooked the Srinagar–Leh highway was back with the Indian Army.

Subedar Mohinder Singh was awarded the Maha Vir Chakra. His citation reads:

Subedar Mohinder Singh was commanding a platoon of a battalion of Punjab Regiment in an attack on a well-fortified enemy post supported by medium machine guns in the Kargil sector. The attack was held up by enemy medium machine guns which were effectively bringing down a heavy volume of fire. He exhorted and inspired his men by personal example to maintain momentum of the attack. With utter disregard for his personal safety, he charged forward, destroyed one of the medium machine gun bunkers and inflicted casualties on the enemy in close combat. His personal example and gallantry so inspired his men as to ensure success of the attack. Throughout, Subedar Mohinder Singh displayed conspicuous gallantry and leadership.

The Tribune

Maj. Chewang Rinchen, MVC
and Bar

'LION of Ladakh' is a title that perfectly fits Col Chewang Rinchen. He was decorated in all the four wars he fought in his Army career—in 1947–48, 1965 and in 1971 against Pakistan, and in 1962 against China.

Born in 1930 at Sumur village in Nubra valley north of Leh, he exhibited attributes of bravery very early in his life. When Pakistan began the invasion of Kashmir in October 1947, Ladakh was in grave jeopardy from the Gilgit–Baltistan raiders from the north. Chewang was in the tenth standard, studying at Leh, when he learnt that Pakistani raiders, having reached Zojila, were heading towards Leh. Another axis for the raiders to reach Leh was via Gilgit–Skardu–Turtuk through Nubra.

He was a little short of eighteen at the time. He trekked back to his village and gathered twenty-eight volunteers, named them 'Nubra Guards', and reported to the nearest Army post at Turtuk to join the fight to stop the intruders from entering the valley.

After a short basic training, the Nubra Guards joined the 7th J&K Militia. Sepoy Rinchen's leadership qualities were quickly recognized and he was promoted to the rank of Jemadar.

Soon enough, he was to receive the Maha Vir Chakra, becoming the youngest to get the second highest gallantry decoration. His citation reads:

In September 1948, Jemadar Chewang Rinchen of 7th J&K Militia, while negotiating a height of 17,000 feet under heavy snow and extremely inclement weather, led the charge by the 28 Nunus (Ladakhi term for the young ones) onto the intruders and recaptured the tactically important Lama House from the enemy in Nubra sector.

In another daring action, having marched for three days through heavy snow blizzards, he launched a fierce attack on the most dominating feature near Biangdangdo and captured it. This action was immediately followed by the capture of Tukkar Hill, the last enemy bastion in Leh tehsil, which involved crossing of a snow-clad mountain over 21,000 feet. During the last action, half of his platoon was suffering from frostbite but under his inspiring leadership and following his example of personal bravery, his men accomplished the seemingly impossible feat.

For his daring act of taking on the enemy far superior
in number, and recapturing the lost ground, Jemadar
Chewang Rinchen was awarded the Maha Vir Chakra.

On 1 June 1959, Subedar Rinchen, MVC, was granted
Temporary Commission and was posted to 14 J&K Militia
as Second Lieutenant. In the 1962 India–China conflict, he
was awarded the Sena Medal for leading a rescue patrol near
Chandni Post in Daulat Beg Oldi (DBO), Ladakh. During the
war with Pakistan in 1965, Captain Chewang Rinchen was
mentioned in dispatches for his role in defending the territory
in Nubra valley, which he had recaptured in 1948.

In 1971, as a Major, he led a company-sized group called
the 'Dhal Force' against a strongly held Pakistani post on Point
18402. After a bitter fight, the force successfully recaptured
the post and also the tactically vital Chalunka complex. Seeing
the enemy in hasty retreat, he captured almost 800 sq. km
of the Turtuk area, which was in illegal occupation of the
Pakistan army.

For this daring operation against all odds, he was awarded
the Bar to the Maha Vir Chakra (the award won a second time).
The battle account reads:

Major Chewang Rinchen of Ladakh Scouts was the
commander of the force assigned the task of capturing
the tactically vital and strongly held Chalunka complex
of the enemy in Partapur sector north of Leh. The
complex consisted of nine strongly held positions,
each fortified with mine and wire obstacles. Major
Rinchen planned and executed the operation with
professional competence and great zeal. Under most

adverse weather conditions, Major Rinchen led his men displaying aggressive spirit and cool courage, moving from bunker to bunker, exhorting and encouraging his men to destroy the enemy, making the operation a complete success.

Chewang Rinchen retired from active service in 1980. However, on popular recommendation, he rejoined the Army in 1983 in the rank of Lieutenant Colonel. Before his final retirement in 1985, he was conferred the honorary rank of Colonel.

The Tribune

Capt. Devinder Singh Ahlawat (Posthumous)

A third-generation soldier, Devinder Singh Ahlawat was born in Gochhi village of Rohtak district of the then undivided Punjab in 1947. After a year in Government College, Rohtak, he joined the NDA and was commissioned into the 10th Battalion of the Dogra Infantry Regiment in 1967. The 10 Dogra is proudly referred to as 'Terrific Tenth'.

During the 1971 war, it was of vital importance to eliminate the Pakistani enclaves at Dera Baba Nanak and Sulaimanke to prevent Pakistan from using them as launch pads for any offensive against India. The 10 Dogra and 71 Armoured Regiment were tasked to capture the east end of the Dera Baba Nanak bridge near the enclave, which was heavily fortified.

Capt. Devinder's company had to clear the most formidable link bundh in the second phase. Capt. Devinder led his company from the front and cleared the supposedly impregnable bundh, which cost him his life, but it was a sacrifice for the ultimate cause and in the best traditions of the Indian Army. Capt. Devinder Singh Ahlawat was awarded the Maha Vir Chakra, posthumously. His citation reads:

During the 1971 India–Pakistan war, 10 Dogra was tasked to capture Dera Baba Nanak bridgehead on the night of December 5/6. As per the battalion attack plan, 'C' company led by Captain Devinder Singh Ahlawat was to capture east-end of the bridge on which the enemy defences were based on a series of concrete embankments with anti-tank guns and heavy automatic weapons. The company, led by Captain Ahlawat, came under heavy machine gun fire from a concrete pillbox. With complete disregard to his life, Captain Ahlawat charged onto the pillbox, grabbed the burning hot machine gun barrel with his right hand and threw a grenade into the pillbox with his left, killing the firing crew, thus making it possible to continue the momentum of the attack and capture of the objective soon thereafter. In this action, Captain Ahlawat lost his life and his body was found with six bullet wounds on his chest, and his hand still clutching the machine-gun barrel.

The Tribune

Lt Col Narinder Singh Sandhu

AN alumnus of Khalsa College, Amritsar, Lieutenant Col Narinder Singh Sandhu had taken over the command of 10 Dogra just a few months before the 1971 war.

The Dera Baba Nanak bridge is a road-and-rail double bridge which sits over the river Ravi and connects several Indian towns with Sialkot and Narowal in Pakistan. The eastern side of this bridge was occupied by Pakistan and was turned into a fortress. It fell upon Lt Col Sandhu to reclaim the bridge.

For his dynamic leadership and bold execution of the attack plan, he was awarded the Maha Vir Chakra. The battle account reads:

On December 5, 1971, 86 Infantry Brigade Group was ordered to eliminate the Pakistan bridgehead across river Ravi, north of Dera Baba Nanak. The area consisted of a series of embankments defended by an elaborate system of concrete defence works housing machine guns, anti-tank weapons and other small arms. 10 Dogra battalion, under the command of Lieutenant Colonel Narinder Singh Sandhu, was allotted the task of capturing the east-end of the bridgehead, which was the hub of the enemy defences in the area. Lieutenant Colonel Sandhu led his battalion most skilfully when the men fought from bunker to bunker to capture the objective. In the bitter fighting, he was seriously wounded in his leg; however, with complete disregard to his own safety, he continued to lead his men with cool courage and determination. His exemplary conduct and inspiring leadership so enthused his men that the vital objective was captured with minimum casualties to the battalion.

The Tribune

Brig. Krishnaswamy Gowri Shankar

THE Commander of 86 Infantry Brigade, Brig. Krishnaswamy Gowri Shankar, was originally from the Corps of Signals. For his boldness and originality in the planning and execution of the offensive in the Dera Baba Nanak battle in 1971, he was awarded the Maha Vir Chakra. His citation reads:

> Brigadier Krishnaswamy Gowri Shankar was commanding an infantry brigade which was responsible for the defence of Dera Baba Nanak on the Western Front. His brigade was given the task of capturing a well-prepared and heavily fortified enemy locality, which was held in strength by the enemy. He showed boldness and originality in the planning of the attack. During the attack, he was always in

the forefront, directing operations and exercising personal control, undeterred by heavy enemy tank, medium machine gun and artillery fire. By his presence with the forward troops, sharing their hardships and dangers, he not only inspired confidence but also was able to modify the plans to ensure speed and maintain the momentum of the attack. His skill and inspiring presence ensured success of this attack with heavy losses to the enemy. During this action, Brigadier Shankar displayed conspicuous gallantry and outstanding leadership.

The Tribune

Lt Col Rattan Nath Sharma, Brig. Anant Vishwanath Natu, Lt Col Harish Chandra Pathak

O N a Christmas eve in the Punjab countryside, a speeding car ran over a man waiting at a bus stop. What a way it was to go for the old soldier of Naked Hill, who was once at the centre of India's own little 'forever war'.

Lt Col Rattan Nath Sharma was commanding the 21st battalion of the Punjab Regiment forty years before he was mowed down by the car, far from Nangi Tekri—Naked Hill— which he had snatched from Pakistan on 11 December 1971. The height, at 4,665 feet in the Poonch sector on the Line of Control (LoC), is a complex of three hills. It was called Nangi because its peaks were incongruous in their barrenness despite the vegetation all around them. Sharma's MVC citation reads:

> His battalion was assigned the task of capturing an important enemy locality situated on a dominating feature. This was a well-prepared locality held in strength by the enemy. During the assault, the enemy brought down intense artillery and small arms fire, inflicting heavy casualties on our troops. Undeterred and with complete disregard for his personal safety, Lieutenant Colonel Sharma encouraged his men and by his presence and cool courage inspired them to achieve the objective.

Some of the men, moving up in two flanks of 21 Punjab's Alpha and Bravo companies, used their bodies as shields for their comrades. Some others bayoneted their way to the top after crawling through minefields. Rattan Nath Sharma himself did all of this to take the height from the defended Pakistani post. It was a classic infantry offensive.

Nangi Tekri has never known peace since.

In the air action during which an IAF MiG-21 piloted by Wing Commander Abhinandan Varthaman went down in PoK (and he was captured and released), Pakistani jets had targeted the post in February 2019. In the October 2016 'surgical strikes' on suspected terror bases, Nangi Tekri was one of the posts from which Indian special forces launched their offensive. In 2013 and 2017, there were beheadings of Indian soldiers, followed by 'punitive artillery shelling' in the vicinity of the post.

What the Nangi Tekri action, along with similar actions, did achieve was a change in semantics: in the 1972 Simla

Agreement that followed the December war, the nomenclature of the Ceasefire Line (CFL) was changed to 'LoC'.

That was to a large extent because of the defence put up by the Poonch (93) Brigade (till recently one of the largest in the Indian Army) commanded by Brig. Anant Vishwanath Natu.

Natu's role in 1971 was also acknowledged by Pakistani experts. Mostly surrounded by dominating heights, Poonch was aggressively targeted by the Pakistan army's 12 Division. It was 'a bold gamble undertaken with insufficient resources', and it failed because of 'the refusal of the Indian brigade commander to panic', wrote AH Amin.[1]

Natu began observing Pakistani movement early on, before the hostilities were declared on 3 December, and redeployed his forces in four sub-sectors, and particularly for two heights, Gulpur and Banwat. Natu's MVC citation reads:

> The enemy launched a massive attack on the night of December 3, 1971 with two infantry brigades supported by three artillery regiments against the brigade sector. Thereafter, for four days and nights, the enemy repeatedly attacked the Gurpur and Banwat features held by his brigade. Brigadier Natu planned, organised and conducted the defences with great skill and professional competence. Cool and collected, this officer inspired his command with exceptional courage and total disregard for his personal safety and repulsed enemy attacks. In the process of heroic defence of the

---

1 'The Western Theatre in 1971: A Strategic and Operational Analysis', orbat.com

Poonch sector, his brigade inflicted heavy casualties on the enemy.

On the same day that the action at Nangi Tekri in the Poonch sector climaxed, further south, in the Shakargarh Bulge, the 'tongue' of territory held by Pakistan that threatened Indian communications between Jammu and Pathankot, Lt Col Harish Chandra Pathak's 8 Sikh Light Infantry took the Pakistani post at Fatehpur. The MVC citation for the officer, who rose to be a Major General, said:

Colonel Harish Chandra Pathak's battalion was given the task of capturing Pak Fatehpur, a well-fortified position held in strength by the enemy. During the attack, the enemy brought down intense and accurate artillery and small arms fire on the assaulting troops, inflicting heavy casualties. Lieutenant Colonel Pathak with complete disregard for his personal safety and displaying rare courage moved forward and led the charge and captured the objective after a fierce hand-to-hand fight. The enemy launched two fierce counter attacks. Lieutenant Colonel Pathak's men beat back the enemy attack, inflicting heavy casualties.

In this action, Lt Col HC Pathak displayed conspicuous gallantry, exemplary leadership and devotion to duty in the best traditions of the Army.

Sujan Dutta

Lance Naik Drig Pal Singh (Posthumous), Sepoy Pandurang Salunkhe (Posthumous), Maj. Dharam Vir Singh, Rifleman Pati Ram Gurung (Posthumous)

INFANTRY, it is said, is the last 100 yards of a nation's foreign policy, necessarily executed by the foot soldier. So it was in most instances in the 1971 war, too.

Lance Naik Drig Pal Singh was called upon to deliver Indian foreign policy near Fazilka (Punjab). His bust now adorns a war heroes' memorial at Asafwala in Fazilka district, where the remains of more than eighty other Indian soldiers that were found after the war are interred.

Seen from Pakistan, the area around Fazilka is flat. But when Maj. Shabbir Sharif, leading 6 Frontier Force's Bravo company, strode up a hastily built observation tower around the middle of November 1971, he could see an Indian battalion position to be reached by the Beriwala bridge about 7 kms inside Indian territory.

He sent a Lieutenant forward with a section. They surprised the Indians and took the bridge intact. That bridge would be returned only at the end of the war, but not before a dramatic shoot-out between Sharif himself and an Indian company commander, Narain Singh.

The details of the encounter are still hazy, just like the dust it raised. But we will run with the popular version that even as Sharif shot Narain Singh, the Indian hurled a smoke grenade that seared the Pakistani. Singh was shot, and Sharif was burnt in the face. Singh was out of the battle, though whether he was killed instantly or died being transported to a hospital is vague. Sharif lived to fight another day. But just one more day.

He was killed from machine gun fire from an Indian tank. Singh's troops had just got reinforcements. Lance Naik Drig Pal Singh of 15 Rajput was among them. He would deliver the infantryman's foreign policy. This is how he did it as the head of a section, not at the Beriwala bridge, but at the Ghazi post, on a flank that was in support of the Pakistanis, as his MVC citation describes:

Even after the capture of the objective by the battalion, two enemy medium machine guns in pillboxes were still interfering with the reorganisation and inflicting casualties on our troops. Realising the importance of silencing these guns, Lance Naik DP Singh took two other ranks with him and with utter disregard for his life and safety crawled up to the first bunker and silenced the medium machine gun by lobbing a grenade. He then started crawling to the next bunker but in the process received a burst from the machine gun on his left shoulder. Although bleeding profusely, he crawled to within 6 feet of the second bunker and was about to lob a grenade when he received a second burst of automatic fire in his chest, killing him on the spot. His daring act, however, forced the enemy to abandon the second bunker, leaving behind the machine gun and a large quantity of ammunition.

An aside is merited here: Shabbir Sharif was awarded Pakistan's highest wartime honour, the Nishan-e-Haider. Decades later, his brother Raheel Sharif rose to be the army chief, now retired.

India could not recapture Beriwala bridge, which was returned after the war for exchange of territory elsewhere. The battle in Fazilka was somewhat of a reversal for the Indian Army in the western front, even as its foot soldiers did their bit. But what Sepoy Pandurang Salunkhe of the 15 Maratha Light Infantry did would have been unbelievable, if not for the many eyewitness accounts that were collated later.

In the battle of Burj, north-east of Amritsar—in a sector where 15 Infantry Division was in a 'holding' position—the Pakistanis of 42 Baluch had pushed the BSF back from two posts early on 3 December.

The 15 MLI had to recover them and go from a defensive to an offensive position by 4 December. The Pakistanis did not push ahead. Also, a company of East Bengal Rifles decided around that time to cross over. They wanted to go to East

Pakistan to help the Mukti Joddhas. Having crossed over to the Indian side, they shared valuable intelligence on the Pakistani dispositions.

The Indians now decided to attack in strength. This was done by the Ganpats—as the Maratha soldiers were called—along with a troop of Vijayantas from the Armoured Regiment. The 'integrated' force advanced, routing 43 Baluch. But one rocket launcher (RL) detachment held out. Salunkhe's MVC citation describes what happened:

> Realising the danger to our tanks, Sepoy Pandurang Salunkhe, at great risk to his life, charged towards the rocket launcher, jumped on the enemy and physically snatched away the rocket launcher even though he received a burst of stengun fire at pointblank range. In this action, Sepoy Salunkhe displayed indomitable courage and determination of a very high order.

(An aside: 43 Baluch was disbanded by the Pakistan army after the war).

Further north, in the Shakargarh Bulge, the last bits of foreign policy got stuck in mud, lost in tall grass, and pirouetted with tanks in little circles that churned up heroes in the Battle of Basantar before being rolled back.

The 'tongue' of Pakistani territory that licks at the Pathankot–Jammu highway continues to be Pakistani. Among the many skirmishes (battles) inside it was one for the battle of Chakra, a Pakistani position that was determinedly holding out.

Major Dharam Vir Singh's 8 Grenadiers were tasked to take it. The initial forays to take it from the front had been defended.

In a change of tactics, Vir Singh was asked to go behind the position with his men.

Major (later Col) Singh had the assistance of 9 Field Engineers (Sappers) to carve a way through minefields and a squadron of tanks from 4 Horse.

The taking of the position was easier than its defence. Maj. DV Singh's citation, describing the fight against four waves of counter-offensives that took place, reads:

> A battalion of the Grenadiers was given the task of capturing a heavily defended enemy position at Chakra on the Western Front. During the attack, the enemy brought down intense artillery and small arms fire, inflicting heavy casualties on our troops. Major DV Singh, commanding the left forward company, undaunted by enemy fire and his depleted strength, led his company through a minefield and by personal example and exemplary courage inspired his men to rush to the objective and capture it after a fierce hand-to-hand fight. The enemy subjected this position to heavy artillery bombardment and launched a counter-attack in strength on December 11. Major DV Singh, with utter disregard for his personal safety, moved from trench to trench encouraging his men and motivating them to stand fast and repulsed the attack inflicting heavy casualties.

Ten days before the Major took the Pakistani position at Chakra, Rifleman Pati Ram Gurung from Lamjung in Nepal had already delivered Indian foreign policy in classic fashion—that, too, before hostilities were formally declared.

On November 30, this soldier from 5/1 Gorkha Rifles was tasked with his medium machine gun detachment to hold a position overlooking a road that the Pakistanis would take for reinforcements. This was in the eastern front.

The Rifleman was already a war veteran, having seen action in 1965. Gurung's citation reads:

> His company was attacked by intense and accurate heavy machine gun fire from an enemy bunker. Rifleman PR Gurung immediately rushed forward and single-handedly charged at the enemy machine gun post. Though mortally wounded, he continued the charge and silenced the enemy machine gun before he fell down dead. In this action, Rifleman PR Gurung displayed outstanding bravery in total disregard for his personal safety.

The Rifleman had rolled a grenade, the gridded iron ball, into the Pakistani position before being killed in action. Gurung, having fought in two wars, was only twenty-three years old.

Sujan Dutta

Lance Naik Nar Bahadur Chhetri and Assistant Commandant Ram Krishna Wadhwa (Posthumous)

WHEN Gen. Andre Beaufre landed at Delhi's Palam Airport with his wife in early 1972, the Frenchman was met by members of the liaison cell of the Indian Army's Military Intelligence Directorate. He was suggested an itinerary by the Army, but he asked to make his own plans.

Beaufre, a military theoretician and French army officer, was invited by Gen. (later Field Marshal) Sam Manekshaw to visit India. Reason: Beaufre had spent days with the Pakistan army during the 1971 war on India's western front around the Shakargarh Bulge and Chhamb. During his tour, Beaufre was given, among other presentations, a sand model understanding of the Battle of Chhamb that has for decades now been a

favourite subject of study in the Indian Army. India had won
the war but had lost that battle.

On his return to Paris, Beaufre sent Manekshaw a note.
In it, recalls PR Chari in his paper, 'India's Finest Hour', for
the Institute of Peace and Conflict Studies to commemorate
Manekshaw, Beaufre said that the Indian Army's operations
in East Pakistan (Bangladesh) were manoeuvre warfare, an
'engineers' war', and the sinking of the Pakistani submarine the
PNS Ghazi (off the coast of Vizag) was a 'stroke of luck for the
Admiral' (Krishnan, then Eastern Naval Command chief). And
he disparaged India's operations on the western front, calling
them, euphemistically, a 'creeping offensive'.

India's operations on the western front were literally the
last few hundred yards of its diplomacy. Through the months
preceding the war, Prime Minister Indira Gandhi had toured
the globe, persuading the bipolar Cold-War world of the time
that she was most concerned about the refugee exodus from
East Pakistan, where Rawalpindi's Generals were persecuting
Bengalis, while India did not really want to push itself in the
west.

Nar Bahadur Chhetri of the 12th Battalion of the Brigade
of the Guards was with its Charlie ('C') company at Mandiala
in 10th Division's area of responsibility in the sector west of
Jammu. This was the same area where, six years earlier, India
and Pakistan had fought bitterly in the stalemated war of 1965.

The Munnawar Tawi near the ceasefire line of the time
flowed down south to meet the Chenab. The land here is
undulating, often with tall 'sarkanda' grass, and the waterways
fordable—tank country, in military terms. The town or large
village of Chhamb, dominated by Hindus, was to the west of
the Tawi.

Chhetri and his anti-tank platoon from 12 Guards (then an infantry battalion, now mechanized infantry) were on guard at the Chhamb, crossing over the Munnawar Tawi, when their commanders erred in judgement. The 10 Division top echelons had assumed that they should be in defensive positions till Manekshaw visited the formation just before the hostilities began.

'Don't lose the Chhamb salient,' he had dictated to them. The Chhamb salient was a launchpad of sorts inside the Pakistani territory. The evening of the same day that the PAF bombed Pathankot and other airbases on 3 December in the morning and formally initiated hostilities, Pakistan artillery started bombarding Indian positions.

Shortly after 8 a.m. the next day (4 December), the Indians saw Pakistani Sherman tanks attempting to cross into the Indian 191 Brigade area under Brigadier RK Jasbir Singh. Neither the Pakistani nor Indian tanks at the time were equipped with night vision devices. They manoeuvred mostly early in the morning.

The Indian side had laid minefields, but had left a gap through which its own forces could go into Pakistani territory. But between the time that the minefields were laid and the battle broke out, the division had re-oriented from a defensive deployment in depth to an offensive one. That left the defences in depth areas weak. A post-mortem study suggested that the commander should have taken both exigencies into account in planning his deployments.

The Pakistanis infiltrated through the Dewa-Ghopar axis, and as the assault troops began fording the Tawi, the anti-tank guided missiles (ATGM) platoon began firing. According to Nar Bahadur Chhetri's MVC citation,

On December 4, 1971, the enemy launched a massive attack with a combined force of infantry and armour. Lance Naik Chhetri's position was subjected to intense artillery mortar and automatic fire by the enemy. With complete disregard for his personal safety, Lance Naik Chhetri engaged the enemy and knocked out five enemy tanks. In this action, Lance Naik NB Chhetri displayed conspicuous gallantry and devotion to duty in keeping with the highest traditions of the Army.

His gallant action, however, could not prevent the fall of Chhamb. That was a consequence of 'ineffective and indecisive command and control', according to Maj. Gen. Sukhwant Singh in his book, *India's Wars since Independence*.

That Pakistan's breaking through the defensive line at that juncture did not result in greater lapses on India's part was largely because the Pakistani divisional commander, Maj. Gen. Iftikhar, was killed in a helicopter crash.

Beaufre, the French General, who was in Pakistan mapping the war even as it was being waged, and was later invited to India, did not delve too deeply into the battle because he said that both sides were exaggerating claims. He used his experience to later develop theories of conventional war in a nuclear shadow. (Neither Pakistan nor India had conducted nuclear tests yet at the time, but the world was in the grip of the Cold War led by the US and Soviet blocs).

However, diplomacy continued after the Indian reversals on the battlefield of Chhamb. The Pakistanis celebrated the capture of Chhamb by hoisting their flag atop its tallest structure and promptly renamed the place Iftikharabad after the General who planned their tactics but did not outlive the battle.

A little over six months later, in the Simla Agreement, Pakistan retained Chhamb in exchange for India's retention of the territory north of Kargil that it had captured in the 1971 war. India also released 93,000 prisoners of war, captured mostly from East Pakistan.

In the battles that waged before the release of prisoners, however, the diplomacy of Mr Grenade—whose word no one trusted once the pin was pulled—carried on on the western front, going on to claim the life of Assistant Commandant Ram Krishan Wadhwa of the BSF in the Punjab–Rajasthan area, making him the first police officer to win the Maha Vir Chakra.

The Battle of Chhamb, despite the heroism of Lance Naik (later Subedar Major) Nar Bahadur Chhetri, a Gorkha from Boorali village in Nepal, took the heaviest toll on the Indian Army in the war. An estimated 400 soldiers were killed, 723 were wounded, 190 went missing or were taken prisoner, and eighteen tanks and other vehicles were lost.

Wadhwa was in charge of two Border Outposts (BOPs) that were at first overrun by the Pakistan army after heavy artillery fire on the night of 4–5 December. His BSF troops had to vacate the posts, and while they were retreating, according to an unofficial account, they were fired upon by Indian troops who mistook them for Pakistanis.

Wadhwa was ordered to re-occupy and retain Raja Mohtam Post, which he did at the cost of his life. Even after the recapture, a superior Army officer was wounded in a mine blast and had to be evacuated.

Wadhwa's MVC citation reads:

The Border Security Force picket at Raja Mohtam near Mamdot on the western front had been occupied by the enemy on December 5, 1971. Shri RK Wadhwa, Assistant Commandant, was assigned the task of recapturing it. He led his troops gallantly through heavily mined area and under intense and accurate fire. His courage and personal example inspired his men to close in on the enemy and capture the objective. Later, when he was counter-attacked, he showed exemplary courage and utter disregard for his personal safety in going from trench to trench encouraging his men in repulsing the enemy. However, while moving under heavy fire, he was mortally wounded by enemy shelling and succumbed to his injuries.

In this action, Assistant Commandant Ram Krishna Wadhwa displayed exemplary courage, leadership and indomitable spirit and devotion to duty of a very high order.

Sujan Dutta

Group Capt. Chandan Singh

As 57 Mountain Division, 23 Division and 8 Mountain Division, under Maj. Gens Ben Gonsalves, RD Hira and KV Krishna Rao, found themselves on the east banks of the rivers Meghna and Surma, their Corps Commander Lt Gen. Sagat Singh was searching for innovative solutions to seriously threaten Dacca by the end of the first week of operations in his 4 Corps zone. Turning to his IAF Task Force Commander Group Captain Chandan Singh (later Air Vice Marshal), he remarked, 'Chandan, do what you have to, but get me into Sylhet and across the Meghna river to put pressure on the Dacca Garrison. If there is a window of opportunity, I want to be the first into Dacca.' If there was anyone in the IAF who could match up to Sagat's energy and his ability to convert operational ideas into outcomes, it was his fellow Rajput, Chandan Singh.

Commissioned as a fighter pilot, a serious accident on a Spitfire during an emergency landing in 1949 almost wrote off Chandan's flying career. Determined to get back into the cockpit, he soon commenced flying Dakotas and then the C-119 Packet before converting onto An-12s just as Ladakh was flaring up in the early 1960s. Squadron Leader Chandan Singh led the air-dropping missions over Ladakh to sustain forward posts and came back with his aircraft riddled with nineteen bullet holes on the first day of the 1962 conflict; he then flew in tanks to the Chushul airfield. Awarded a Vir Chakra for his exploits in the 1962 conflict with China, Group Captain Chandan Singh was already a legend in the IAF's transport fleet when he was called upon to perform extraordinary feats during the 'Lightning Campaign' in December 1971.

Chandan's exploits in the 1971 conflict saw him wearing two hats and demonstrating organizational brilliance and personal courage. As the Station Commander of Air Force Station, Jorhat, he was entrusted by Air Chief Marshal Lal with setting up the Kilo Flight, the forerunner of the Bangladesh Air Force. Manned by a few select pilots, including Group Captain Khandker and Flt Lt Sultan Mahmud (both future Air Chiefs in the Bangladesh Air Force) and airmen who had defected from the PAF, a few accomplished IAF helicopter and transport pilots were chosen to clandestinely train them. Among them was Flying Officer Karandikar (later Air Commodore), who recalls his association with Chandan Singh with awe and reverence. He recalls that the team was equipped with the Dakota, the slow-moving Otter aircraft and Alouette helicopters, with the Otter and Alouette modified for weapon delivery and armed with rocket pods, and a machine gun operated by a gunner firing sideways out of an open-door hatch. Chandan shifted them to Dimapur, a satellite base, from where they gained proficiency in night flying and weapon delivery before they were moved to Kumbhigram and then forward to Kailashahar in early December to support the 4 Corps operations.

Karandikar recalls flying the Dakota solo on a few occasions as he flew some fuel and armament stores from Kumbhigram to Kailashahar, an unconventional decision which only a risk-taker like Chandan would authorize. Chandan Singh's magnanimity was evident when he ensured that the Bangladeshi pilots were given the opportunity of firing the first shot at the enemy on 3 December as he tasked the Otter with a rocket attack on the oil tanks at Narayanganj, and the Alouette to attack the oil tanks at Chittagong just after midnight. Chandan often flew with the Kilo Flight and they did a great job throughout the campaign by flying missions at night against several targets.

Encouraged by the Kilo Flight's initial success, Lt Gen. Sagat Singh agreed to Chandan's suggestion that Kailashahar, right on the Tripura-East Pakistan border, should emerge as the aviation hub of Sagat Singh's 4 Corps, and Chandan Singh was unofficially re-designated as the Task Force Commander. This is where Chandan Singh wore his second hat as the orchestrator of the first ever large-scale heli-landed operations in independent India, if one discounts the heli-landed operation at Aizawl during the Mizo insurgency of 1966. Strategizing extensively with Sagat at 4 Corps HQ in Teliamura, Chandan soon had a large complement of battle-proven Mi-4 helicopters from the 110 Helicopter Unit (HU) at Kailashahar, supplemented by a few IAF and Army Alouette light helicopters. While the former were primarily troop carriers, the latter would prove immensely useful in the recce and scout roles.

Responding to the first call to action, Chandan Singh himself flew a mission to Sylhet on the morning of 7 December to investigate reports from Indian Army intelligence that the Pakistan army wanted to surrender. Met with a fusillade of machine gun fire and receiving several hits on his Mi-4 helicopter, Chandan reported back to Sagat that it was a trap. Reacting coolly, Sagat asked Chandan whether he could cross the Surma river and land a battalion under fire, and seize the initiative by surprising two Pakistani brigades, which would be anticipating a larger conventional assault by several brigades. The rest is history, as 110 HU heli-landed 4/5 GR commanded by Lt Col Harolikar under fire at the gates of Sylhet in a display of spectacular jointmanship. Supported by airstrikes by IAF fighters and the Kilo Flight under Forward Air Controller (FAC) control and receiving continuous waves of Mi-4s, the Gorkhas fought valiantly for over a week, preventing the Pakistani brigade from reinforcing Dacca and coercing it sufficiently to surrender on 16 December.

Emboldened by the success of the Sylhet operation, Sagat urged Chandan to push his weary helicopter crew, who had flown non-stop for over forty-eight hours, to heli-land several brigades of 57 and 23 Division at multiple points across the wide and mighty Meghna river by 13 December. Relocating to Agartala, 110 HU was reinforced with more helicopters and crew from two more units to cope with the volume of lifting an entire brigade with its complement of engineers and light artillery to chosen landing zones at Raipura, Narsingdi and Narayanganj from the divisional forward HQ of Brahmanbaria. The 4 Guards was the second unit after 4/5 GR to participate in the operation, and it came out with flying colours despite hardly any preparatory time for the operation. Here, again, leading from the front emerged as a key force multiplier, as Sagat and Chandan Singh insisted on carrying out the first recce of the proposed landing ground at Raipura in a Chetak helicopter. Flying into heavy ground fire, the co-pilot was shot through the leg, and over thirty bullet hits to the helicopter were counted after the sortie. Executing a series of crossings, the helicopter task force landed over two brigades on the west bank of the Meghna in an operation that is termed as 'vertical envelopment'. By doing so, they cut off any possible reinforcement routes to Dacca from the other garrisons and facilitated a multi-pronged advance that forced the surrender of Dacca.

While the pilots and crew of 110, 105, 111 HU, Kilo Flight and the Chetaks performed magnificently during the nine-day relentless operation, the 4 Corps battle was a commanders' battle, with the senior leadership leading from the front. Complementing the drive of Sagat, Ben Gonsalves, Krishna Rao and Hira, Chandan Singh proved to be the ideal air commander who understood the land battle as no one else did. For his exceptional leadership in multiple operational tasks, personal courage, daring risk-taking ability and motivational charisma, Group Captain Chandan Singh was the senior-most IAF officer to be awarded the Maha Vir Chakra during the 1971 war.

Air Vice Marshal Arjun Subramaniam (Retd)

Wg Cdr Vidya Bhushan Vashisht

WING Commander Vidya Bhushan Vashisht (later Air Vice Marshal), among the most experienced An-12 pilots in the IAF at the time, assumed the command of 44 Squadron in August 1971 under trying circumstances. The squadron had just lost its commanding officer and an entire crew in an accident while practising a live bombing mission, and restoring morale and getting the squadron battle-ready was uppermost in the mind of Vashisht. Thus emerged the story of how an An-12 squadron under a dynamic commanding officer covered itself with glory in the western sector during the 1971 war. No stranger to 44 Squadron, having been the flight commander of the unit, Vashisht knew all the crew and personnel of the unit intimately. With an able and proactive flight commander, it was not long before the squadron was ready for battle.

Honing its bombing skills and modifying the delivery platform with a bomb cradle for each 500-lb bomb, which was designed by an Army officer, the squadron moved to Bareilly in Central Air Command a few days before the war commenced. With a maximum bomb load of forty such bombs, a six-aircraft mission packed quite a punch of TNT (trinitrotoluene). The IAF's bomber force was concentrated between Bareilly, Agra and Gorakhpur to relieve the pressure on the Western Air Command, a wise move as it allowed the planners to centrally coordinate all bombing missions from one headquarters.

Group Captain Gursaran Ahluwalia (then a Squadron Leader and flight commander of the squadron) had a ringside view of the transformation of the squadron into a feared bomber unit during the 1971 war, particularly on the western front. He recalls Vashisht as

a quiet and inspirational leader, an exceptional flyer, organizer and a coolheaded and kind person. I never saw him losing his nerve and he always had a pleasant smile on his face. He was exceptional in understanding the abilities of men under his command and had implicit faith in me as his No. 2 and left all the planning, briefings and debriefing to me.

Vashisht led the opening night bombing missions over the Changa Manga forest on the nights of 3 and 4 December 1971. Intelligence reports had indicated that the area had a large ammunition dump and large troop concentrations. Dropping his bomb load from low levels itself, Ahluwalia recollects that the sky was lit up with the explosions, and that both Pakistan Radio and Pakistani newspapers reported the raid and its effects the next day. Over the next two weeks, the squadron flew around forty-five missions against a variety of targets, which included a Pakistani artillery brigade at Haji Pir Pass that was harassing Indian operations, a divisional headquarters at Fort Abbas, the Sulaimanke bridge, a railway yard at Hyderabad, and the Sui gas plant. There was also a cheeky day raid on Skardu airfield with Canberra bombers on the last day of the conflict. By all reports, the night raid over Haji Pir and the day raid over the Sui gas plant, also flown by Vashisht and Ahluwalia, proved to be the most effective of all. While the gas plant was seen to be burning for several days after the raid, the air and army chiefs personally rang up to congratulate the squadron for the successful Haji Pir raid.

While most of the raids comprised six aircraft, the Skardu airfield raid on 12 December involved only one An-12 acting as a pathfinder-cum-lead bomber for the Canberras. Without taking away any credit from the Canberras, the comfort levels of the An-12 squadron in flying over mountainous terrains prompted the Central Air Command to assign Vashisht to lead the formation. Seeing their success in the west, the squadron was also assigned to target a large ammunition dump near Dacca on 13 December, a mission that was led by Ahluwalia. Vashisht's inspirational leadership and good teamwork ensured that no aircraft or crew was lost during the entire conflict, though Ahluwalia recollects three missions in which his aircraft was damaged by ground fire. He was even chased by a PAF Mirage-3, which had locked on to him and was probably seconds away from firing a missile. It was an alert IAF fighter controller, Sqn Ldr ML Bauntra, who saw this on the radar screen and yelled at Ahluwalia on the open channel to duck down to tree-top level, a warning that saved the aircraft and crew—such are the bomber tales from 1971.

Describing the mission profiles with remarkable clarity, Ahluwalia recalls,

> For the day raid on the Sui gas plant, we flew from Bareilly to Jodhpur, refuelled there and then flew at 300 feet and got down to 100 feet approximately 150 miles from the border. A minute before the target and at speeds of slightly over 500 km/hr, we pulled up to 300 feet, dropped our bombs and got back to 100 feet till we entered Indian territory. For the Haji Pir night mission, we flew directly from Bareilly to Srinagar at 20,000 feet and descended to 6,000 feet over Srinagar airfield; we then navigated to Poonch airfield and further on to Haji Pir, returning via the same route after bombing the Pakistani brigade.

The pilots were responsible for accurate navigation to the target area, situational awareness, and the evasive action to be taken to avoid ground fire or any ongoing aerial threat. The navigator assisted the pilots in the navigation and also used the improvised gun sight to decide the right moment to release the bombs, before which the rear door was opened; the tail gunner and flight signaller would then come into action as they would first activate the fuses and then allow the cradles to slide out of the rear doors even as the pilots pitched up the nose and accelerated the aircraft for the bombs to fall under the force of gravity. While 44 Squadron has the distinction of being the first transport squadron to have been awarded with Battle Honours by the President of India, Squadron Leader Gursaran Ahluwalia and his navigator from the squadron, Flight Lieutenant PB Kalra, were awarded Vir Chakras. Wing Commander Vidya Bhushan Vashisht was awarded the Maha Vir Chakra for his intrepid and daring leadership of 44 Squadron through the conflict. Excerpts from his citation reveal much:

On the night of December 5, 1971, he led a formation of his bombers, this time to attack enemy positions in the Haji Pir Pass in Pakistan-occupied Kashmir. The difficulties and dangers of this operation were due as much to the great volume of ground fire in the target area, as to the hazards of flying his large aircraft and leading his formation at low level through mountainous terrain. Wing Commander Vashisht pressed home the attack and achieved marked success in hitting the enemy's positions. In addition to these, he led many other missions deep into enemy territory where opposition could be expected from fighter aircraft and anti-aircraft fire. In all these raids, Wing Commander Vashisht completed the tasks assigned to him without any loss to our aircraft. He displayed inspired leadership, exceptional devotion to duty, and conspicuous bravery in repeatedly leading attacks against heavily defended enemy targets, night after night.

Air Vice Marshal Arjun Subramaniam (Retd)

Wg Cdr Swaroop Krishna 'Suppi' Kaul

SOON after he took over the command of No. 37 Squadron (Black Panthers) at Hasimara (an airbase in North Bengal) in April 1971, Wing Commander Swaroop Krishna 'Suppi' Kaul (later Chief of Air Staff) was asked by the Senior Air Staff Officer in the Eastern Air Command, Air Vice Marshal Devasher, to explore the possibility of modifying the Hunter Mk 56s to carry photo-recce pods. This was considered a key operational requirement to create a mosaic of ground deployments of the Pakistan army in East Pakistan. Soon after, the Black Panthers were chosen for this additional role since Suppi had a lot of experience in Fighter Reconnaissance (FR) with cameras on Vampires.

Accordingly, from May to June 1971, around six fighter aircraft and a trainer of the squadron were modified with

Vinten cameras, two side-looking F-95 cameras and a forward-looking one, the F-135, in the nose. As soon as the trainer was ready, Suppi trained a few pilots in this role. Harish Masand, a young Flying Officer, was among these pilots and emerged as Suppi's near-permanent wingman from then on till the end of the war, collecting a Vir Chakra for his own individual exploit of shooting down a Sabre on the first day of the war on 4 December in a chaotic dogfight and melee over Dacca.

By October 1971, Suppi and Harish were doing FR missions inside East Pakistan, photographing areas/targets of interest. That is when Harish gathered how good Suppi was at low-level navigation. As his wingman, Harish's job was to keep abreast of him around 2,000 yards and keep the tail of the formation clear while they navigated to the target, and then let the cameras roll from both aircraft when he called. Almost from the first such mission over hostile territory, Harish realized that he did not ever have to look at the map: if a check point was to be crossed at seven minutes and fifty seconds, he just had to glance at the ground at that time, and the check point would be right where it was supposed to be. Due to Suppi's accurate navigation and gentle corrections in course/speed in total radio silence, Harish could devote a major portion of his attention to scanning the skies around and behind for any enemy threat. That is how he spotted two Sabres well in time on the very first mission on 4 December 1971, and that is a story that Harish has narrated earlier.

Suppi and Harish did some nine FR missions before the war, the last one being as late as on 2 December over Comilla and Lalmai Hills for 4 Corps. Taking off from Guwahati, they landed in Kumbhigram (Silchar) around noon because they did not have the gas to get back. The photo section in Kumbhigram developed the films, 6,000 frames between the two of them, after which Suppi and Harish stayed up till 2 a.m., looking at the photos and marking out gun positions, troop concentration and the defensive works on each frame with a Chinagraph pencil, since there was no photo interpreter available, and the intelligence was required urgently by the Army. The films were sent off to the 4 Corps headquarters in Teliamura the following morning (3 December) before they flew back to Hasimara to get into the war the very next day.

Suppi flew several strike missions during the war, including the mission that struck the Governor's House in Dacca on 14 December, but his risk-taking and leadership qualities emerged on Day One itself. Harish recounts that mission with clarity.

We were to launch the first raid of four Hunters on Tejgaon airfield on December 4, call sign Mission 501, Time Over Target of 0705 IST/0735 East Pakistan Time. The formation comprised Suppi in the lead, Billoo Sengar as his wingman, Mascarenhas as number 3 and me as number 4. Suppi's aircraft did not start so he jumped into the standby aircraft. Mascy's aircraft went unserviceable so we took off as three aircraft. After take-off, my landing gear refused to go up and I started trailing the lead section of Suppi and Billoo for quite some time till I finally decided to use the emergency override switch and get the gear up and catch up. While I was having this problem, Suppi could have easily aborted the mission since two of the four aircraft had fallen out, but he continued, displaying his courage and dedication to the task given to him. Fortunately, we finally went in as three aircraft since we were bounced by two F-86 Sabres about two minutes short of target and had to engage them in combat.

Throughout the war and the many missions we did together, Suppi was cool and did not ever flinch from facing the heavy anti-aircraft fire over Dacca or the threat of enemy Sabres during the initial days of the conflict. He was also open to suggestions from youngsters like me on the planning of missions and attacks, which resulted in great team effort for more effective attacks with minimum losses. Due to adaptation of different attack patterns through such open discussions between us, we survived the war without a scratch, at least when we were together, even in the attacks on Governor's House in Dacca on 14 December and the university area on 15 December wherein the anti-aircraft fire was dense.

Suppi was also a compassionate human being during the war and cared about his subordinates, officers or men. I personally experienced how he handled the loss of my younger brother, a paratrooper, during the war when the unfortunate news came to him on 10 December. Slowly, and very gently, he broke the bad news to me and told me to get drunk that night and take the next day off, an offer that I firmly declined.

Wing Commander Kaul was awarded the Maha Vir Chakra for leading his squadron into battle. The citation said, 'His reconnaissance flights over Tejgaon and Kurmitola airfields, in the face of the most sustained and heavy enemy ground fire, stand out as acts of heroism, extreme gallantry and devotion to duty.'

Modest and gracious as ever, Air Chief Marshal Swaroop Krishna Kaul attributes the performance of the squadron to exemplary teamwork and esprit-de-corps.

Arjun Subramaniam and Harish Masand

Wg Cdr Padmanabha Gautam, MVC and Bar

THE Canberra fleet of the IAF is a proud one. Its contribution by way of its bombing role in Congo, in the two India–Pakistan wars of 1965 and 1971, and in the recce roles in 1962 and in Kargil is outstanding by any yardstick. We celebrate the accomplishments of one of the two IAF Canberra pilots who are recipients of the Maha Vir Chakra twice over, Wing Commander Padmanabha Gautam, Commanding Officer of the 16 Squadron during the 1971 conflict. (Wing Commander JM Nath is the other).

Gautam took over the command of 16 Squadron, also known as the Black Cobras, in November 1969. He had just returned from Iraq after a welcome instructional assignment that had followed a hectic six years of flying and achievement. He was also part of the IAF Canberra contingent in Congo in the early 1960s. As the CO of the Jet Bomber Conversion Unit (JBCU), a Canberra squadron in 1965, he was awarded his first Maha Vir Chakra for the several risky missions that he flew as a pathfinder to hit targets at the extremities of the Canberra's radius of action, such as Peshawar. Not satisfied with that, he executed a near dead-stick landing in Iraq on a MiG-17 while on deputation to the Iraqi Air Force as an instructor, for which he was commended by both the Iraqi government and the IAF. Air Marshal Vir Narain, one of the pioneer navigators from the Canberra fleet and several years Gautam's senior, remembers him as a confident, cocky and very competent young pilot.

Two navigators from the squadron, Wing Commanders Ranganathan and Group Captain Dutta, had a ringside view of Gautam's tenure as commanding officer from two different perspectives. While Wing Commander Ranganathan, now in his late eighties, was a Squadron Leader, a few years junior to Gautam and his navigation leader in the squadron, Group Captain Dutta was a Flying Officer with three years of service, who still talks about his former CO with awe. Training and bonding for over two years under Gautam made the Black Cobras a formidable unit as war clouds loomed on the horizon in mid-1971. Gautam was an addicted flyer, according to both Dutta and Ranganathan, and wanted to be in the cockpit whenever the opportunity presented itself. Dutta recollects that though 16 Squadron, based in Gorakhpur, was primarily assigned with roles in the eastern theatre of operations, Gautam's experience in the western sector in 1965 prompted Air HQ to assign the squadron with several missions in the west, too.

Reflecting the systematic approach to training and preparing for war that had permeated through several squadrons of the IAF in the build-up to December 1971, Gautam created pilot-navigator teams that commenced training as early as in March 1971. Choosing abandoned World War II airfields in Uttar Pradesh, Bihar and West Bengal as simulated targets, the squadron perfected the art of low-level ingress at night into hostile territory at 500 feet, popping up to 7,000 feet for weapon delivery, which comprised dropping 8X1000-lb bombs, and then diving down to 300–500 feet for the perilous return leg home. Being the senior-most among the commanding officers of the three Canberra squadrons, Gautam was often called to Allahabad, the HQ of the Central Air Command, where all mission planning was done.

Remembering his former CO as a fun-loving family man with a great sense of humour and a love for music, who wore his accomplishments lightly on his shoulders and drove around in his Mercedes Benz, Ranganathan recollects that from early November 1971 onwards, Gautam made it a point to engage with all his aircrew on issues such as courage, bravery and fear. Everyone in the Black Cobras knew who would be the one to fly the riskiest missions and that leadership under fire would never be an issue.

Dutta recollects that Gautam and he were an inseparable pilot–navigator pair as they initially undertook night bombing missions in the western sector over Mianwali airfield and the Raiwind railway marshalling yard near Lahore. Three or four aircraft would get airborne from Gorakhpur, land at Ambala to refuel and arm before striking targets and returning to Gorakhpur in the wee hours of the morning. All the missions faced a hostile reception over the target area as the sky would be invariably lit up with ack-ack fire, and it was through a combination of skill and luck that the squadron suffered no losses in the western sector. Shifting focus to the east once the IAF had achieved air superiority, 16 Squadron commenced its attacks on targets in Chittagong, Khulna and the military cantonment on the outskirts of Dacca. The squadron got hit on the last day of the war when they lost the effervescent Flight Lieutenant Brian Wilson and his navigator Flight Lieutenant Mehta over Dacca in a day raid over Kurmitola.

Gautam and Dutta flew together on six long-distance and long-duration missions as the squadron clocked almost seventy operational missions during the war. Dutta particularly remembers a night mission to Mianwali, where they dropped jelly-filled spike bombs that were innovative runway denial weapons. It was later confirmed by one of the Bengali pilots of the PAF based at Mianwali, who escaped to India via Afghanistan, that a PAF F-86 Sabre was destroyed while trying to scramble without realizing that there was jelly and spikes on the runway. Dutta was awarded a Vir Chakra for being an ideal foil to Gautam, who himself was awarded a Bar to the Maha Vir Chakra for his inspirational leadership of the squadron and personal exploits of sustained courage and flying skills in war.

Moving to Pune as the chief operations officer (OC flying in those days), on promotion to Group Captain, Gautam flew both the MiG-21 and the Canberra there. Unfortunately, he perished in a MiG-21 crash on 25 November 1972 after his aircraft flamed out after take-off. A school located close to the Air Force station still commemorates that day with a silent prayer in remembrance of Gautam, as he is believed to have steered the stricken MiG-21 away from the school where it was directly headed for impact. In the process, he lost critical seconds that would have facilitated an ejection. Gautam's courage and selflessness had followed him from the war zone, and he will remain an inspiration for future generations of the IAF.

Air Vice Marshal Arjun Subramaniam (Retd)

Wg Cdr Cecil Parker and Sqn Ldr Ravinder Nath Bhardwaj

BY the time of the 1971 Bangladesh liberation war, 20 Squadron of the IAF, the Lightnings, was well prepared. Its CO, then Wing Commander Cecil Parker, had been in the role for over two years. He had previously founded the Operational Training Unit (OTU) of the IAF, trained on the same Hawker Hunter aircraft that the Lightnings were now operating, and had been Lightning flight commander. With over 1,000 Hunter-flying hours, he was one of the most experienced IAF Hunter pilots of the time.

The squadron also had a solid flight commander in Squadron Leader Jal Mistry. In addition, as part of the strengthening of all units in preparation for the war, they had an experienced supernumerary, then Squadron Leader Ravinder Bhardwaj, on attachment. As it happens, he was a course mate of Sqn Ldr Mistry's, had himself been flight commander of the Lightnings earlier, and had served under Wg Cdr Parker in the OTU as well.

Other personnel had been rigorously trained and exercised, and knew what was expected of them. Everyone knew that war was coming; the Lightnings knew their targets, and had prepped carefully for each one.

So when the shooting started, with the attempted Pakistani pre-emptive strike on the evening of 3 December, the squadron was as ready as could be. There was just one tiny snag—most of the aircraft and pilots were not at their base that evening.

For some time previously, with full expectation that war was imminent, IAF squadrons at forward locations intermittently withdrew their aircraft to rear bases. On the evening of the Pakistani strike, 20 Squadron's aircraft and personnel were scattered between Ambala and Hindon, their previous base.

They would start flying into Pathankot early next morning. But the squadron's orders for the next day's counter-strikes arrived overnight. And the first one had a Time Over Target of sunrise Pakistan time, which meant that the mission would have to take off well before dawn in India. Their own aircraft would not be back in time.

Undaunted, the squadron launched its first two missions before dawn, using aircraft borrowed from the co-located 27 Squadron. Wg Cdr Parker, 'exercising his prerogative', as the squadron diary noted, led the squadron's first foray into enemy territory, with then Flight Lieutenant Charan Singh 'Channi' Dhillon as his No. 2.

That first mission, with Peshawar as the target, was one of the longest-range strikes undertaken by single-engine, single-seater aircraft during India–Pakistan wars. During the 1965 war, the PAF had treated Peshawar as their safe harbour and had withdrawn their most valued assets there during the night.

That 1971 morning, at high speed and at low level, Parker and Dhillon hooked around Peshawar so as to approach unexpectedly from the west rather than from the east. They executed two passes, hitting a Sabre being refuelled from a bowser and a fuel installation before exiting. They were pursued by three or four Pakistani Sabres, who, over a long chase, were able to gradually catch up. Because of the fuel and aircraft configuration, the Hunters could not engage in combat and had to simply jettison their auxiliary tanks and fly hell for leather. The Sabres were able to close in and fire, and managed several hits on the Hunters. Wg Cdr Parker called for a tactical break, timed such that his No. 2 would be breaking in the direction of India. One Sabre, unable to stay with Parker's tight turn (his g-counter showed he had pulled 10g), overshot. Wg Cdr Parker emptied his remaining ammunition on that Sabre, catching it squarely in his sights as confirmed by his gun-camera films. Unfortunately, he did not have enough shells left to bring the Sabre down, having nearly emptied his cannons over Peshawar itself. By then he was almost at the border, and the Pakistanis gave up the chase.

Parker and Dhillon approached Pathankot, eking out the last few miles literally on fumes. Wg Cdr Parker was cleared for a straight-in approach, and his engine flamed out immediately on landing. Flt Lt Dhillon's engine actually flamed out while still in the air, but skilled airmanship brought him and his Hunter safely down to a dead-stick landing. Both aircraft were back from the squadron's first mission with tanks completely dry, and peppered with bullet holes.

The squadron settled, if that can be said of wartime, to a stern but matter-of-factly executed routine of about twenty sorties a day. Most of its pilots flew at least one sortie into the enemy territory each day. They endured two losses, one on that first day itself, of the young and always smiling Flying Officer KP Muralidharan. The other was the following day, their trusted Flight Commander Squadron Leader Jal Mistry lost to missile-armed PAF Mirages while (successfully) attacking the ferociously-defended PAF Operations Centre at Sakesar.

The squadron continued its assigned counter-air role over the next few days, striking enemy airfields. One of their targets was Chaklala, the airfield for Rawalpindi, where they destroyed a few light transport aircraft—one of which, as it turned out, was the personal aircraft of Brigadier-General Charles 'Chuck' Yeager, the United States Air Force (USAF) Second World War ace and jet-era test pilot, who was at this time a military adviser to the US Ambassador to Pakistan. Yeager's reaction was said to be one of fury, but it was mocked and turned into laugh-out-loud funny accounts by both a US diplomat serving alongside him in Pakistan and by the Lightning pilot responsible for that demonstration of accurate gunnery under fire.

Another memorable counter-air strike, led by Sqn Ldr Bhardwaj, was on Murid, a new airbase in Pakistani Punjab, where five enemy aircraft were destroyed in a single strike. Bhardwaj and his formation actually only claimed to have destroyed two; the full toll they had exacted was confirmed in Pakistani accounts later.

Yet another spectacular strike was on an economic target: the Attock oil refinery, one of only two refineries in Pakistan at the time. The squadron diary describes, and numerous photos confirm 'towering sheets of orange flames, and billows of oily black smoke' from the installation.

After five days of non-stop raids, mainly on enemy airfields, the Lightnings turned to a different task: close air support (CAS) for the Army at Chhamb. As is well known, the Chhamb sector, where the geography favours Pakistan, and where the Pakistan army concentrated skilfully in twice our strength, was where the Indian Army was hardest pressed during the war. CAS was needed, and the Lightnings, based close by, flew nearly a dozen sorties each day for the next few days in support of the troops on the ground.

One morning during that period, Sqn Ldr Bhardwaj was leading a CAS pair orbiting over Munnawar Tawi, hampered by the early morning mist common in the north Indian winter, when his wingman, Flying Officer BC 'Lofty' Karambaya, spotted two Pakistani Sabres firing at him. Flying Officer Karambaya has shared a detailed account of this. He describes using the Hunter's flaps to turn tighter than his pursuer while calmly remaining in continuous R/T contact with his leader even as a few shells hit his Hunter. When Bhardwaj confirmed visual contact, and not before, Karambaya broke east. The Sabre tried to follow, but Sqn Ldr Bhardwaj had caught up, and opened fire. The Sabre exploded in an orange fireball, giving Sqn Ldr Bhardwaj an air-to-air kill, still an iconic token of air superiority.

In talking to former Lightnings years later, I found that their collective pride in the squadron's successes is clear. Air Vice Marshal (as he later became) Parker is always quick to turn the conversation to the officers and the men he commanded, and to highlight the squadron's wider accomplishments.

Among the Lightnings that year was a young Indian Navy aviator, then Lt Arun Prakash, doing the regular exchange programme with the IAF that many IN aviators do. He went on to significant career accomplishments himself, rising eventually to Chief of Naval Staff. In later years, both AVM Parker and Admiral Prakash had occasion to speak in public on leadership and war. Interestingly, each invariably paid tribute to the other. The respect is clearly mutual, and has lasted these fifty years.

At the end of the war, Parker and Bhardwaj (who later became Air Marshal) both received Maha Vir Chakras. AVM Parker will be the first to say that his decoration is an honour not only for him personally, but also for the team he led. The twenty-eight officers and 300-odd other personnel under his command bore themselves to become one of the most highly-decorated units in the armed forces. Apart from the two MVCs, the squadron received five VrCs (including for Sqn Ldr Mistry, Lt Prakash and Fg Off. Karambaya) and numerous other honours.

KS Nair

Sqn Ldr Madhabendra Banerji and Wg Cdr Allan Albert D'Costa

THEY used to say that he saw better blindfolded. Squadron Leader Madhabendra Banerji was among the first batch of pilots from the IAF trained to fly the Sukhoi-7 fighter bomber in what was then Soviet Russia. 'There is nothing as good as total darkness for navigation. Try being a blind person and you will know,' Banerji recalled his instructor telling him, two years before the 1971 war.[1] As Squadron Leader (later Air Vice Marshal), Banerji was based in Adampur, close to and north-east of Jalandhar. He was flying bombing missions to provide close air support to the land battles in the Shakargarh sector.

---

1   Source: Anchit Gupta, bharat-rakshak.com

The many battles in the Shakargarh bulge, in part a consequence of a change in strategy of an Army formation from offensive to defensive, often blurred the lines for both the Indian land and air forces. The Army often called for close air support, which was tasked to Banerji's squadron, among others.

Air Chief Marshal PC Lal, who was Chief of Air Staff in 1971, writes in his book, *My Years in the IAF*, about the operations at Shakargarh:

> ... although adequate air effort was available, the right kind of targets were not identified. The Sukhois were large aircraft that could be spotted from a great distance and despite packing quite a punch, whenever they delivered rockets against Pakistani armour, they proved to be quite vulnerable to ack-ack (anti-aircraft) guns and came out second-best when engaged by PAF F-86 Sabres and F-6s in aerial combat, losing three aircraft in battle.

At another point in the book, he recalls pilots telling him that the situation in Shakargarh was so confusing 'that it is difficult to distinguish between friend and foe'.

In his own squadron—101 Falcons—whose flight commander he was, Banerji experienced the vulnerability his Air Chief later wrote about. One of his pilots was shot down over no-man's land. The pilot ejected, broke a leg, but limped to a sparse forest to hide. Hours later, a 1-tonne with soldiers came to him; both he and the soldiers were suspicious of each other, unsure as to whether they were encountering friend or foe. The soldiers turned out to be Indian. The Captain leading them verified this by asking him for passwords. The pilot was transported to Adampur first, where Banerji met him, before he was sent onwards to be hospitalized in Delhi.

Banerji's own attempts to initiate night flying with the Su-7 got mixed responses from air headquarters at first. But he did fly late in the night/early in the morning of 4 December, hours after Pakistani aircraft had attacked Indian airbases and war was formally declared. Strangely, the Su-7 flew most of its missions in daylight.

'When war happens, human behaviour changes,' Banerji would often repeat to his trainees when he was an instructor. In an interview to Bharat Rakshak, Banerji acknowledged later that implementing night-flying drills was quite a task.

In the coming months, the letter from Air Headquarters came clearing one squadron in each command to do the night-flying syllabus. The Command gave the task to 26 Squadron, but the squadron did not have their heart in it and did not really utilise the opportunity to its potential, resulting in suboptimal results.

My CO in 101 Squadron, KC Khanna, got the go-ahead from WAC (Western Air Command), and he gave the task to me. We started the task and had initial difficulties, but slowly we started to make it work. While we could not get the entire squadron operational, but most of the senior pilots had got operational. Simultaneously, TACDE (Tactics and Combat Development Establishment) was formed and moved to Adampur and they were actively testing out night flying too. Sure enough, as soon as the war began, TACDE put in night flying to full use and they were the only force to reach Sargodha and were effective.

Banerji's MVC citation reads:

> Squadron Leader M Banerji, a senior pilot in a fighter bomber squadron, led no fewer than 14 missions within the first week of the conflict with Pakistan against enemy targets, most of them in support of our Army in the Chhamb battles. During these missions, Squadron Leader Banerji destroyed two enemy tanks and two guns. On these occasions, Squadron Leader Banerji was personally responsible for attacking the enemy in the face of heavy ground fire, thus relieving pressure on our own troops. Squadron Leader Banerji displayed conspicuous gallantry and skill in repeatedly attacking enemy forces in the face of extremely heavy ground fire.

Banerji and his senior from another squadron, Wing Commander Allan Albert D'Costa, were among the first pilots to be trained in the Sukhoi-7 and were required to train others. D'Costa was in fact the leader of the first batch that was trained in Soviet Russia in 1968.

Wing Commander (later Group Captain) D'Costa was the officer designated to induct the Sukhoi-7 aircraft, a new acquisition, into the IAF.

For months before the outbreak of the war, D'Costa was both priming the aircraft that were being flown into India from Russia and training the flying and ground crews. The day after the formal outbreak of hostilities, he flew a low-level photo recce over Pakistan's Walton airfield and located their radar unit. He conducted repeated strikes over the Risalwala and Chander airfields and took out three tanks in Christian Mandi.

Lal wrote in his book:

No. 222 (Tigersharks) Squadron led by Wing Commander D'Costa flew against the airfield at Risalewala near Lyallpur on December 4 (from Halwara) in the morning and later gave close support at Sulaimanke and further north along the river at Hussainiwala and Dera Baba Nanak and Narowal in the Shakargarh Bulge.

D'Costa's MVC citation reads:

On December 4, 1971, Wing Commander AA D'Costa, the commanding officer of a fighter bomber squadron, was the first to strike at the enemy's Risalewala airfield. Next day he led a mission to Christian Mandi and destroyed three tanks. The following day he led an attack on a concentration of tanks at Dera Baba Nanak, notwithstanding intense anti-aircraft fire. On December 7, he carried out a low-level photographic reconnaissance mission in the Sulaimanke area. He followed this up by leading an attack on the same day on the railway station at Narowal, where he personally destroyed and damaged many railway wagons and some installations. Thereafter, he flew a number of reconnaissance missions, bringing back a large volume of intelligence and other missions against railway marshalling yards and Raiwind and the Kasur-Lahore railway track, destroying a large number of wagons and causing devastation at each target in the face of intense anti-aircraft fire, and against Pakistani air opposition. Throughout the operations, Wing Commander D'Costa displayed conspicuous gallantry, determination, leadership and professional skill.

Sujan Dutta

Wg Cdr Ramesh Sakharam Benegal and Wg Cdr Harcharan Singh Mangat

CHIEF Lynx looked down at the watery-green carpet below and swooped low from over Kamalpur in northern East Pakistan, shortly after the hostilities broke out on 3 December 1971. Taking off from Tezpur, he had flown a circuitous route to avoid detection by Pakistani radars. The terrain was all too familiar.

The chief of the 'Lynxes' squadron was Ramesh Sakharam Benegal, then a Wing Commander and Commanding Officer of the 106 Squadron, flying the English Electric Canberras on bombing and photo-reconnaissance runs.

In an earlier life, Benegal was in jail, incarcerated by the British for being a member of Subhas Chandra Bose's Indian

National Army (INA). The Japanese had selected him for training at the Imperial Japan Air Force Flying Academy during World War II, on account of which Benegal was called 'Tokyo Boy' by some of his associates.

A natural choice for the IAF, Benegal deployed his men and flew missions himself over Karachi before the naval raid that took out the Pakistan port city's fuel dumps, and also to inspect the damage after the Battle of Longewala.

Benegal's life was quite dramatic, spanning tumultuous times. The thread that runs through it is a yearning for adventure and Independence for India. He had participated in World War II, in India's freedom movement, had been jailed by the British, and finally had a career in the IAF. He wrote a book, *Burma to Japan with the Azad Hind,* on his time with Bose's INA. This book gives us a glimpse into the ideas that Benegal cherished and the values that he brought to the service. (He also inspired the biopic on Bose by his nephew, Shyam Benegal.) Subhas Chandra Bose, aka Netaji, visited the academy in Japan where Benegal had been seconded to be trained by the Imperial Air Force, he writes. In 1944, Bose was scheduled to visit the academy. The Indian cadets, each of whom had a portrait of Bose in his room, were all agog with excitement. Benegal writes in his book:

We were made to stand in front of our rooms as Netaji had expressed his wish to meet each of us individually. We all had photographs of Netaji in the INA uniform in our rooms and took the golden opportunity of having them autographed by him. Signing forty-five photographs on a visit like this was time-consuming, but he did it patiently and with a smile.

Netaji spent at least two minutes with each cadet and asked about each one's welfare. When he came to my room, he astounded me by telling me that my brother Sumitra was in the Rangoon Headquarters and was quite well. He then asked me if I had received any letters from him and when I replied that no one had written me any letters, he said that he would remind Sumitra to write to me. He then signed my photograph and moved on to the next room. I have since held responsible posts as a commanding officer and I know what it means to an individual when a superior officer remembers his name and anything about his family...

In a sense, Benegal was used to danger and hardship since he was in his teens. Born in Rangoon (Burma, now Myanmar), he and his mother tried to flee the country when he was just fifteen, and failed. Months later, he became acquainted with Bose and the INA. He sailed to Singapore to sign up with Azad Hind Fauj. He was seconded to train with the Japanese, but the vessel on which he was travelling was torpedoed and he landed up in the Philippines. After Japan's surrender in the War, he fetched up in Madras. He was imprisoned by the British and was one of those accused of treason in the Red Fort INA trials, but was released by the authorities, who increasingly feared the consequences of taking action against people like him as the freedom struggle in India gathered momentum.

Unlike most of his contemporaries, Ramesh Benegal brought to the Indian military a flavour that did not have its origins in the Royal IAF, but a tradition of an independence movement that was largely eclipsed by the imposition of an idea of what is 'mainstream'. But the values he brought saw him lead a squadron that operated in both the eastern and western theatres of the 1971 war.

Benegal's MVC citation reads:

> As the commanding officer of an operational reconnaissance squadron, Wing Commander RS Benegal carried out a large number of missions over enemy territory and obtained vital information about enemy air force and other installations. The missions entailed flying deep into enemy territory and to heavily defended targets. The information brought back from these missions facilitated the planning of Army, Air Force and Naval operations and thus directly contributed to the attrition of the Pakistan war machine. It is further to the credit of Wing Commander Benegal that he never returned from any of these innumerable missions without having achieved his objective in full measure. While flying repeatedly deep into enemy territory, Wing Commander Benegal displayed conscientious devotion to duty and professional skill of a very high order.

The Su-7 hero

The aircraft with tail number B858 sits today in the museum of the IAF at Palam, Delhi, repainted in its original camouflage colours. It was Harcharan Singh Mangat, Commanding Officer of the No. 32 Squadron, who once famously flew the plane.

He is still known as the man who flew a jet which had a missile rocketing into it but did not explode.

Wing Commander (later Air Cmde) Mangat was flying the Sukhoi-7 on 4 December 1971—a day after the PAF attacked Indian airbases and formal hostilities were declared. On 3–4 December, within hours of the Pakistan air strikes on Indian airfields, there were 118 counter-air sorties on Pakistan airfields by the IAF, which included, apart from the Sukhoi-7, MiGs, HF 24s and Hunters.

Wing Commander Mangat of the Thunderbirds (32) Squadron was flying the Sukhoi-7, newly imported from Soviet Russia, when a Sidewinder missile from a Pakistan Air Force J6 jet rammed into his aircraft. Before that, ground anti-aircraft fire in East Pakistan had chewed away at his plane's rudder and ailerons. Mangat limped back to base in Amritsar.

This feat led to new survivability studies on the aircraft.

Mangat's MVC citation reads:

As the Commanding Officer of the fighter bomber squadron, Wing Commander Harcharan Singh Mangat undertook a number of interdiction and close support missions, as also many reconnaissance sorties, deep into enemy territory, bringing information of great value to the Army and the Air Force in their operational planning. While on a strike mission, his aircraft was hit thrice by intense anti-aircraft fire but he pressed forward until he found that the other aircraft in his formation had also suffered serious damage. At this point, enemy interceptors came on the scene. Despite this, he extricated his formation from the hazardous situation and led it safely back to base. On landing, it was found that his aircraft was extensively damaged.

Only superb flying skill enabled him to bring a badly damaged aircraft back to safe landing. Wing Commander Mangat displayed conspicuous gallantry, determination, professional skill and leadership of a very high order.

Sujan Dutta

Wg Cdr Man Mohan Bir Singh Talwar

O N 31 October 1984, Prime Minister Indira Gandhi was assassinated. In the pogrom against the Sikhs that followed, from 1 to 4 November, India's capital went into a spiral of violence and killing. Group Captain Man Mohan Bir Singh Talwar (retd) was caught in the maelstrom.

The mobs surrounded his house in West Patel Nagar; they went up the roofs of adjacent buildings and pelted stones and fireballs. Talwar was determined to save himself and his family.

He had a licensed shotgun. He told his sons to wield lathis. The fingers that were so used to wielding the joystick in bomber planes now held the gun and fired into the air. Talwar was arrested and jailed. He was released months later, upon the intervention of people who knew him and also of his gallantry in the 1971 war.

The attacks on Man Mohan Bir Singh Talwar, who died in May 2019, were documented by many, among them British author Pav Singh in his book, *1984: India's Guilty Secret.* 'Talwar appealed to their (the mob's) sense of patriotism by informing them of his military service. That gang was persuaded to disperse by Talwar's Hindu neighbours, who stood by the family throughout the ordeal. However, it wasn't long before a second, larger crowd formed outside Talwar's gates,' writes Singh.

In the IAF, Talwar is known as the man who bombed Sargodha in Pakistan. In 1971, he was the Commanding Officer of the No. 5 'Tuskers' Squadron based in Agra. The official history of the IAF records that the English Electric Canberras of his squadron 'struck hard and deep in December 1971, virtually against the same targets in Pakistan as they had in September 1965'. Talwar was a veteran of the 1965 and the 1971 wars.

Hours after the PAF struck Indian airfields on 3 December 1971, Wg Cdr Talwar and his men took off in their Canberras from Agra, where the runway had been damaged.

'They took off at 2150 hours despite home base Agra having been attacked an hour earlier. Led by the CO, No.5 squadron's first counter-air missions were against the PAF airbases at Sargodha and Shorkhot Road,' the IAF history reads.

Talwar flew to both the western and eastern sectors (West Pakistan and East Pakistan). He had divided his squadron into four batches for its missions.

On 8 and 9 December, his squadron flew five sorties to Chhamb, three to Raiwind, and two to the Jassar railway yards.

On 10 December, the squadron flew three to Chhamb and three to the Lodhran railway yards. On 13 and 14 December, there were eleven missions. A day later, there were three raids near Dhaka and seven missions to the west by the squadron, and on 16 December, the day the Pakistan army in the east surrendered, the Tuskers flew five missions to Chhamb again.

These were relentless bombing runs.

'The IAF gained complete air superiority over East Pakistan in a few days and flew over 2,300 sorties of fighters, helicopters and transport aircraft', records Arjun Subramaniam in his book, *India's Wars: A Military History 1947-1971.*

Within the first twenty-four hours of the attacks by Pakistan, Talwar flew five missions into enemy territory, over land that was his ancestral home. He allotted targets to each of the four batches of his Squadron of B-58 bomber-interdictor Canberras. He flew with all of them, taking out three of four Pakistani artillery gun positions in Chhamb that were pinning down Indian Army troops.

Talwar was born in April 1931 in Abbottabad, now in Pakistan's North-West Frontier Province. Commissioned as a fighter pilot on 14 October 1953, he moved on to fly bombers.

In 1977, Talwar was promoted as Group Captain and was Air Officer Commanding at the Gorakhpur station. He took premature retirement.

His MVC citation reads:

> Wing Commander MBS Talwar, commanding officer of a bomber squadron, led five day-and-night bombing missions against very heavily defended enemy targets within the first 10 days of operations. He inflicted very severe damage to the Pakistani Air Force installations at

Sargodha. In a daylight mission in the Chhamb area, in support of the Army, he attacked four heavily defended enemy gun positions near the Munnawar Tawi river and effectively silenced three of them, facilitating the advance of our troops in difficult terrain. The bold leadership, tenacity of purpose, flying skill and conspicuous gallantry displayed by Wing Commander Talwar were largely responsible for many a success of his squadron.

Sujan Dutta

Capt. Mahendra Nath Mulla
(Posthumous)

THE daring assault on the Karachi harbour on 4 December resulted in the sinking of two Pakistani destroyers and a minesweeper. The number of Pakistani casualties is not known, but the IN lost 178 sailors and eighteen officers, along with their Captain, five days later.

The biggest setback to the Indian Navy patrolling the Arabian Sea came at 8:45 p.m. on 9 December when *INS Khukri*, an anti-submarine warfare frigate, was torpedoed by *PNS Hangor*, a Pakistani submarine it had been hunting for. The *Khukri* sank within minutes of being struck when nearly 200 officers and men were still trapped below decks.

Capt. Mahendra Nath Mulla remained on the bridge and could have saved himself, but the braveheart had already made up his mind. The *Khukri* disappeared beneath the Arabian Sea within three to four minutes of being hit, with its Captain still on the bridge.

For his outstanding courage and determination and for his supreme sacrifice in the best traditions of the Navy, Capt. Mahendra Nath Mulla was posthumously awarded the Maha Vir Chakra. His citation reads:

Two ships of the Indian Navy under the command of Captain MN Mulla, senior officer of frigate squadron, were assigned the task of locating and destroying a Pakistani submarine in the North Arabian Sea. During these operations on the night of December 9, 1971, *INS Khukri* was hit by torpedoes fired by the enemy submarine and sank. Having decided to abandon ship, Captain Mulla, without regard for his personal safety, supervised the arrangements for the rescue of his ship's company in a very cool, calm and methodical manner. Even at a later stage whilst the ship was sinking, Captain Mulla showed presence of mind and continued to direct rescue operations and refused to save himself by giving his own life-saving gear to a sailor. Having directed as many of his men as possible to leave the ship, Captain Mulla went back to the bridge to see what further rescue operations could be performed. In doing so, Capt Mulla was last seen going down with his ship. His action and behaviour and the example he set have been in keeping with the highest traditions of the Service. Captain MN Mulla displayed conspicuous gallantry and dedication.

The Tribune

Cdr Babru Bhan Yadav

THE first recipient of the Maha Vir Chakra in the Indian Navy was born into a military family of Bharawas village in Gurgaon district of then undivided Punjab (now in Rewari district of Haryana).

Babru Bhan Yadav's father, Maj. Bhagwan Singh, was an Order of British Empire (OBE) awardee in World War I. After graduating from St Stephen's College in Delhi, Babru was selected as a Direct Entry Graduate to the Royal Navy. After four years of training at the Royal Navy College, Dartmouth, and one year as Midshipman onboard HMS Devonshire, he was commissioned in the Indian Navy in 1951.

In 1971, to counter any misadventure by Pakistan, offensive plans had been prepared. The Indian Navy's plan was to strike Karachi on the very day that Pakistan carried out its first act of war.

Pakistan's air force attacked the Indian forward airfields at about 5.30 pm on 3 December. Since it was not possible for the Indian naval forces to arrive at a point which was 150 miles from Karachi to commence the run-in the same evening, it was decided that operations would be launched the following day, on the night of 4/5 December.

On 2 December, Commander Babru Bhan Yadav had been given the command of K-25 Squadron, composed of the task forces of three missile boats—*INS Veer*, *INS Nipat* and *INS Nirghat*. Two days later, the Karachi harbour would be witness to the onslaught and fury of this Killer Squadron. For his conspicuous act of bravery against all odds, Commander Babru Bhan Yadav was awarded the Maha Vir Chakra. His citation reads:

> On the night of December 4, 1971, Commander Babru Bhan Yadav, as Squadron Commander of three missile boats' task force, was ordered to carry out an offensive sweep on the enemy coast of Karachi. Karachi harbour, being strategically important, was heavily guarded by the enemy. With a narrow mouth covered by formidable coastal defence, the harbour seemed impregnable. Notwithstanding the threat of the enemy surface and submarine attack, Commander Babru Bhan, onboard *INS Nirghat*, led his squadron deep into enemy waters and encountered two groups of large enemy warships. Despite heavy fire from the enemy destroyers and at great risk to his personal safety and of his personnel, Commander Babru Bhan fearlessly led his squadron towards the enemy in a swift and determined attack.

In that daring Indian marine assault, two enemy destroyers namely *PNS Khaibar* and *Shah Jahan* and one minesweeper *PNS Muhafiz* were sunk. After completion of the mission assigned to his task force, and before sailing back to Bombay, Commander Babru Bhan bombarded Karachi harbour and set its oil installation ablaze and fearlessly sailed back, leaving the harbour in flames. The attack by the intrepid task force into the lion's den, fearlessly led by Commander Babru Bhan, was acknowledged as a resounding success even by the Pakistan Navy.

Commander Babru Bhan Yadav, MVC, retired as Commodore (equivalent to Brigadier).

The Tribune

Cdr KP Gopal Rao

THE first successful assault on the Karachi harbour produced a Maha Vir not just in Commander Babru Bhan Yadav, but in Commander Kasargod Patnashetti Gopal Rao, too. He was commanding two Arnala-class anti-submarine corvettes, namely *INS Kiltan* and *INS Katchal*.

His MVC citation reads:

A small task group of the Western Fleet carried out an offensive sweep on the enemy coast off Karachi on the night of December 4, 1971. Notwithstanding the threat of enemy air, surface and submarine attack, Commander Kasargod Patnashetti Gopal Rao led his task group deep into enemy waters. Despite heavy gunfire from enemy destroyers, and at great risk to our ships and personnel, Commander Rao resolutely pressed home a determined attack, sinking two enemy destroyers and one minesweeper. After the surface engagement with enemy warships, Commander Rao successfully bombarded the port of Karachi, setting fire to oil and other installations in the harbour.

In this operation, Commander Gopal Rao displayed conspicuous gallantry and outstanding leadership in the best traditions of the Indian Navy.

The Tribune

Lt Cdr Santosh Kumar Gupta

I was fortunate to be a part of the 300 Squadron (comprising the Sea Hawk fighters) during the 1971 war, having been in command since January 1970 as a Lieutenant Commander. Initially, it seemed that the aircraft carrier *INS Vikrant*, with its air squadrons, would not see any action as both the ship and the aircraft were in a poor state of repair. *Vikrant* was non-operational, with one of the four boilers requiring replacement, limiting the speed of the ship to 14 knots, against the designed 24.5 knots.

Consequently, with no possibility of embarked flying, the frontline Sea Hawk squadron was allowed to run down. With no carrier to operate from, the squadron languished, with scarcely any aircraft available for flying and with over twenty fresh pilots. In this situation, the squadron was ordered to move at the end of July 1971 to Madras with six aircraft for exercising with *Vikrant*, which had been sailed to the east coast to avoid any attack on it in case of hostilities.

There was, however, an inevitable and genuine feeling of bonding with the mother-ship on board, with an accompanying sense of belonging. Motivation in the squadron was great all-round. Soon we broke all laid-down procedures, and after a few rollers on the deck, we engaged the wire. Pilots were dropping their hook on 'mother' and honing their deck-landing skills.

It was conveyed to us that despite its limitations in operating, *Vikrant* would form the nucleus of the Eastern Fleet in a potential war. Aircraft spares began arriving, and with them, the aircraft. The ship's movement was kept a secret as it was appreciated that the adversary (submarine *Ghazi*) would be on the hunt for a juicy target. By mid-October, there were 18 Sea Hawks on board, and intense training began.

The exercises included air-to-air interceptions, releasing of weapons on the splash target streamed by the carrier, pre-planned strike sorties against shore targets and recovery of aircraft from carrier-controlled approaches (CCA). Arrested landings and catapult launches in marginal conditions became the norm, with one inflexible rule: no landing on the deck with live ammunition.

The *Vikrant* sailed for Chittagong on the midnight of 3 December when hostilities were declared, with Pakistan having attacked some Indian airfields in the north-west. The Sea Hawks provided the strike force by day, while the Alize could be used for reconnaissance duties day and night. Aerial bombing by the Alize on radar was also possible, with limited success. It was intended to attack Cox's Bazar from 100 miles at first light. There was a three-hour delay as the escorting ships raised an alarm with a positive submarine contact on sonar.

At about 1,000 hours, fourteen armed Sea Hawks were ranged on the flight deck, with four earmarked for air patrol against any possibility of in-coming enemy fighter, and ten Sea Hawks armed with twenty-eight rockets and four 20-mm cannon guns. Of these ten Sea Hawks, eight formed the strike force for Cox's Bazar. Transit was to be always at a very low level, skimming the sea to avoid detection. Complete radio transmission (R/T) silence was observed. After the attack, the formation would proceed to the rendezvous point while re-forming for the return flight to land on 'mother'.

Six Sea Hawks were launched at 3 p.m. the same day at 90 miles with similar armament configuration. Two gun boats and river crafts were sunk. A third strike successfully bombed Chittagong harbour, where a warehouse and three merchant ships adjacent were berthed alongside. These were set on fire by direct hits with eight 500-pound bombs, the thick black smoke which rose a few hundred feet into the air becoming a landmark for Chittagong, seen from 60 miles away for three days!

The next day, attention shifted to attacking the river ports of Khulna, Changla and Mongla. The following day, despite marginal conditions, four Hawks armed with two 500-pound bombs attacked a large building in Chittagong city close to a civil hospital. It had been reported that it housed several Pakistani military personnel attending a meeting. Six bombs landed while one remained unexploded. Extensive damage was caused to the three-storeyed building. The adjacent hospital was left unscathed.

One challenging incident merits recall fifty years later. While on a steep dive-bombing attack (with two 500-pound bombs strapped) on a Chittagong airfield installation, my aircraft was hit by ground fire, causing hydraulic failure at a speed of 420 knots. The flying controls of the Sea Hawk at this speed became heavy, making it difficult to manoeuvre the aircraft. The formation exited the scene after releasing their bombs on the target and then reduced their speed to 250 knots to transit back to the 'mother-ship', and I was the pilot with one unreleased 500-pound bomb.

It was a tense situation. The standard drill in peacetime in such an exigency is to land ashore as it can be dangerous both for the aircraft and, more importantly, for the ship, to recover such an aircraft. Landing on board with an armed live 500-pound bomb could result in an explosion caused by the bomb's inadvertent release on the deck from the jolt experienced on the arrested landing.

To his credit, Captain Swaraj Parkash (CO of *Vikrant*) took a calculated risk to permit the recovery with an armed bomb rather than have me eject from the aircraft over the sea. I was the last to land after burning fuel to reduce the aircraft weight, given the mild wind conditions. Those were long moments for me in the cockpit, but the gamble paid off. In violation of all rules, I hit the deck safely.

In all, about 300 strike sorties were flown by aircraft from *Vikrant* in ten days. Eight Sea Hawks and a similar number of Alize were hit by ground fire. In retrospect, despite the many constraints, *INS Vikrant* and its aircraft played a crucial role in the liberation of Bangladesh. It was my privilege to command the White Tigers during this war.

Rear Admiral Santosh Kumar Gupta (retd)

Capt. Swaraj Parkash

SWARAJ Parkash had a spectacular career in the Indian Navy, beginning as a Sub Lieutenant in World War II and retiring as Vice Chief of Naval Staff almost four decades later, in the rank of Vice Admiral. Parkash, the son of a schoolteacher, was born in Jalandhar (Punjab), where he did his early schooling. He had an excellent academic record and was sent to college at Lahore. He appeared for and cleared the examination for recruitment to Indian Mercantile Marine Training Ship (IMMTS) Dufferin and a career in the merchant navy, but gave up that option and chose to join what was then the Royal Indian Navy.

He specialized in navigation and commanded five ships, heading the Western Fleet and Eastern Naval Command. After his retirement from the Navy, he headed the Coast Guard, rounding off his four-decade-long career in whites.

He played a stellar role as the Captain of *INS Vikrant* during the 1971 war. Parkash assumed command of *Vikrant* in mid-1971, when war clouds loomed over the subcontinent, but a question mark hung over the participation of *Vikrant* in the war. Hobbled by untrained crew, engineering defects and material problems, which directly impacted flying operations, the carrier's availability and deployment posed a difficulty for the naval planners. While the visionary leadership of Admiral SM Nanda and Vice Admiral N Krishnan decided to bite the bullet and deploy the carrier in the main theatre of operations, that is, the Bay of Bengal, from June 1971 onwards, it needed someone of the calibre of Parkash to galvanize the rank and file of the ship and deliver the goods.

Parkash was instrumental in getting the ship going, in backing his engineers to resolve its boiler problems and much else through typical Indian innovation, and in working up his air squadrons to perfection. Almost miraculously, within four months, the carrier and its aircrew were raring to go. Parkash meant business in preparing for war. In the words of the late Vice Admiral BR Chowdhury, who served as Parkash's Chief Engineer at that time, '*Vikrant* got ready for war because of the unique leadership and interdependence which spontaneously developed under a competent, wise and humane Command.'[1]

When the hostilities commenced, *Vikrant* was the centrepiece of the Navy's offensive in the east, and the relentless operations of the vessel's air wing resulted in the destruction

---

1   The quotes in this article are based on personal exchanges the author had with the speakers or taken from *Quarterdeck* 1996, a Navy journal published on the twenty-fifth anniversary of the 1971 war.

of enemy shipping, port infrastructure—particularly in Chittagong and Cox's Bazar—and lines of communication, leading to the strangulation of East Pakistan at sea and contributing to the Pakistani surrender at Dacca.

For his leadership and for the risks he took in operating in hazardous waters close to the enemy coast and yet ensuring an accident-free outcome, Parkash was awarded the Maha Vir Chakra. His comrade during the war and then skipper of *INS Kamorta*, Capt. (later Vice Admiral) MP Awati, described Parkash's feat as 'a masterful display of seamanship and shiphandling'.

One instance of this attribute of Parkash's came to the fore on the afternoon of 4 December 1971, when *Vikrant* was ordered to strike Chittagong. At that time, the other fleet units were on a submarine search-and-attack mission and *Vikrant* had no anti-submarine or anti-air protection. Launching an air attack then would have seemed foolhardy, and many of Parkash's officers advised him against it. After deliberating on it for some time, Parkash said, 'Like bloody hell. I did not come to this point to turn back without attacking. Launch the strike.' Capt. CM Vyas, the Fleet Operations Officer at the time, described the order thus: 'Those were the sweetest words I ever heard. Here was leadership of very exceptional quality.'

This extraordinary respect that Parkash got from his seniors, peers and subordinates is evident even today. Rear Admiral Santosh Kumar Gupta, Commander of the Seahawk squadron during the war and himself a Maha Vir Chakra awardee, describes Parkash:

'Capt. Parkash was a thorough professional. Very mature and stable by nature, he was a person who inspired confidence all round. I was soon to acknowledge that he was an extraordinary Captain who was temperamentally cool and relaxed and ever ready to take prompt action in any emergency. He was a true leader of men. Prior to 1971, there had been seven Captains of repute of *Vikrant* I had served with, and I can say with confidence that he was the most exceptional, and I was indeed fortunate that I saw him at close quarters.'

Parkash's direction officer on *Vikrant*, Lt (later Vice Admiral) PJ Jacob, adds: 'His outstanding qualities of leadership made *Vikrant*, with all her limitations, a well-knit fighting unit and ensured success of operations in the Bay of Bengal. He was indeed the right man for the task.'

While the Navy, at all levels, is about teamwork, some people stand out for their contributions, and Parkash was one of them. 'The right man for the task' was the silent hero of our triumph, and the nation owes a debt of gratitude to his stewardship of *Vikrant* at a critical juncture when the nation was at war.

Cmde Srikant B Kesnur

Cdr Mohan NR Samant

THE eldest of five children of Subedar Maj. Narayan Ramchandra Samant, Commander Mohan NR Samant hailed from Parule village in Sindhudurg district along the Konkan coast in the erstwhile state of Bombay.

After passing his Intermediate (Science) from Wilson College, Bombay, Samant joined the Royal Indian Navy and was sent to the UK for four years' training at the Royal Navy College, Dartmouth. He returned in 1953 as Sub-Lt (Navigator) along with the last batch of Indian executive officers commissioned in the UK.

During the operation deep inside the enemy's backwaters in the eastern theatre during the 1971 war, Commander Samant headed the task force of *INS Palash*, *INS Padma* and *INS Panvel*, which not only neutralized the shore defences, but also set ablaze the oil installation in Khulna, the second biggest in East Pakistan.

Commander Samant, for his conspicuous bravery, was awarded the Maha Vir Chakra. His citation reads:

Commander Mohan Narayan Rao Samant was the senior officer of the force which carried out most daring and highly successful attacks on the enemy in Mongla and Khulna ports. Manoeuvring his squadron through a most hazardous and unfamiliar route, he routed the enemy in Mongla inflicting heavy losses. A bitter fight ensued at Khulna and the force was subjected to incessant air attacks. Two boats belonging to the Mukti Bahini operating with the force were sunk. In utter disregard of his personal safety, the officer not only managed to pick up a large number of survivors, but also persisted with fierce attacks on the enemy with devastating results. Throughout the operations, Commander Mohan Narayan Rao Samant displayed conspicuous gallantry, dedication and leadership.

The Tribune

Lt Cdr Joseph PA Noronha

L T Commander Joseph PA Noronha had joined the Joint Services Wing (present-day NDA) in 1955 and was commissioned in the Indian Navy in 1959. Commanding *INS Panvel*, he was part of the task force under Commander Mohan Samant which attacked Mongla, Chalna and Khulna bays in East Pakistan.

His ship was subjected to incessant air attacks and enemy fire from shore defences. However, Lt Commander Noronha, with total disregard for personal safety, handled his ship in the most competent and fearless manner.

For his conspicuous gallantry, Lt Commander Noronha was awarded the Maha Vir Chakra. His citation reads:

Lieutenant Commander JPA Noronha was in command of INS Panvel which attacked Mongla and Khulna areas during the period 8 to 11 December, 1971. The ship was subjected to incessant air attacks. Lieutenant Commander Noronha handled his ship in the most competent and fearless manner in very restricted waters and effectively engaged enemy positions. Inspired by his personal example, the ship's company fought at close quarters for a prolonged period. His bravery, utter disregard for his personal safety, leadership and untiring energy inspired his men to rise to great heights.

He succeeded in silencing the enemy's shore defences and caused very extensive damage to vital enemy installations. Throughout the operation, Lieutenant Commander JPA Noronha displayed conspicuous gallantry and leadership.

The Tribune

Leading Seaman Chiman Singh Yadav

CHIMAN Singh Yadav was just about sixteen years of age when, after matriculation from Rewari, he joined the Indian Navy as a sailor in 1961. Within seven years, as Leading Seaman, he was a Clearance Diver Class 2 and underwater bomb disposal specialist at the Naval Diving School, Cochin. He also specialized in the use of limpet mines against enemy warships and submarines.

During the 1971 war, Operation Trident, the maritime offensive by the Western Naval Command, altered the dynamics by blasting the Karachi harbour and preventing West Pakistan war efforts from reaching its eastern half.

But before the outbreak of the war, Chiman Singh, now a Leading Seaman, not only trained the Mukti Bahini guerrillas in covert operations, but also led many successful operations deep inside East Pakistan waters.

During the 1971 war in the eastern theatre, Leading Seaman Chiman Singh, for his conspicuous bravery, was awarded the Maha Vir Chakra. His citation reads:

During Operation Cactus Lily, Leading Seaman Chiman Singh was part of the crew of a small naval vessel entrusted with the task of attacking enemy targets in Khulna, Mongla and Chalna bays in East Pakistan. On December, 11, 1971, while on the mission, the vessel was subjected to enemy air attack while operating off Khulna and was sunk. Leading Seaman Chiman Singh was thrown overboard and seriously injured by shrapnel. Simultaneously, the enemy shore defences opened fire at the survivors in water.

Chiman Singh noticed that the survivors, including an injured officer, were finding it difficult to keep afloat. Despite himself being seriously injured, unmindful of his own safety against enemy automatic fire, he rescued and brought all the survivors to the shore. On reaching the shore, not bothering about his own injured condition, Chiman, to make it possible for his two colleagues from being captured, charged at the enemy, exposing himself to the hostile fire.

Leading Seaman Chiman Singh was eventually overpowered and taken prisoner by the enemy. He, however, was released upon the liberation of Bangladesh. His valiant action behind the enemy lines and in the face of perceivably insurmountable opposition was an embodiment of the Indian Navy's core values of duty,

honour and courage and the diving cadre's ethos of
strong will to succeed and surmount all odds.

For his conspicuous act of bravery and display of utmost
courage and determination in the face of the enemy,
Leading Seaman Chiman Singh Yadav was awarded the
Maha Vir Chakra.

Chiman Singh was also awarded the 'Friends of Liberation
War' honour by Bangladesh in 2013. Petty Officer Chiman
Singh Yadav is the only sea warrior below officer rank in the
Indian Navy to have been conferred the Maha Vir Chakra, the
second highest decoration for gallantry in the armed forces.

The Tribune

Notes on the Contributors

NN Vohra is the President of The Tribune Trust. A Padma Vibhushan awardee, he has served as the Governor of J&K (2008–2018), Principal Secretary to the Prime Minister, Defence Secretary, and Home Secretary. He has also been the Co-Chairman of the India–EU Round Table; Chairman of the National Task Force on Internal Security; and Member, National Security Advisory Board.

Lt Gen. SS Mehta (Retd) is a Trustee of The Tribune Trust; a former General Officer Commanding-in-Chief (GOC-in-C), Western Command; and a veteran of the 1971 war (Mentioned in Dispatches). He is a recipient of the Param Vishisht Seva Medal (PVSM), Ati Vishisht Seva Medal (AVSM) and Bar, and Vishisht Seva Medal (VSM). He has also served as the GOC-in-C, Army Training Command, Shimla; Deputy Chief of Army

Staff (Planning & Systems); and Member, National Security Advisory Board.

Adm. Arun Prakash (Retd) is a former Chief of the Naval Staff and ex-Chairman of the Chiefs of Staff Committee. He is a recipient of the PVSM, AVSM, Vir Chakra and VSM.

Air Vice Marshal Arjun Subramaniam (Retd) is a military historian and a former fighter pilot. He occupies the President's Chair of Excellence on National Security at the National Defence College (NDC). He is a recipient of the AVSM.

Lt Gen. Raj Sujlana (Retd) is a veteran of the 1971 Indo-Pak War and a former Commandant of the IMA. He is a recipient of the PVSM, AVSM and VSM.

Manoj Joshi is a veteran journalist and a Distinguished Fellow, Observer Research Foundation (ORF), New Delhi.

Maj. Gen. Randhir Sinh (Retd) is a veteran of the 1971 Indo-Pak War and the 1999 Kargil War. He is a recipient of the Uttam Yudh Seva Medal (UYSM), AVSM and the Sena Medal.

Ajay Banerjee is a Special Correspondent of *The Tribune*, specialising in defence matters.

Cmde Srikant Kesnur and Lt Cdr Divyajot are associated with the Naval History Project.

Lt Col AK Ahlawat is a serving officer who writes on military matters.

Wg Cdr JS Bhalla (Retd) has served as Air Traffic Controller in the Indian Air Force (IAF).

Maj. Ishleen Kaur is a serving officer.

Brig. IS Gakhal (Retd) is a former Commandant of the Sikh Regimental Centre.

Sujan Dutta is a senior journalist and a military affairs commentator who has covered wars in Kargil, Afghanistan and Iraq.

Harish Masand is a retired Air Marshal and a Vir Chakra awardee. He is also a recipient of the Vayu Sena Medal.

KS Nair is an expert in Indian aviation history.

Rear Adm. Santosh Kumar Gupta (retd) is a Maha Vir Chakra awardee of the 1971 war.

Acknowledgements

First as a series of newspaper articles and then as a book, the idea to celebrate the memory of the heroes of the 1971 war remains very dear to The Tribune Trust President NN Vohra and the Board of Trustees. It was indeed a matter of great pleasure and privilege to have received the wholehearted support of some of our best defence writers, not just in contributing to the series and the book, but also in identifying other writers to nurture and strengthen the project. In particular, Commodore Uday Bhaskar (retd) and Air Vice Marshal Arjun Subramaniam (retd) have been extremely supportive. Our in-house defence expert, Special Correspondent Ajay Banerjee, was of great help. Deputy Editor Rahul Puri enthusiastically worked towards getting the articles published and also wrote a substantial number of articles afresh for the book. *The Tribune* Library staff has been responsive to all the repeated requests for clippings and visuals. This book would not have been possible without Assistant Editor Vikramdeep Johal meticulously and diligently poring over the proofs many times over. HarperCollins CEO Ananth Padmanabhan's response made the book a reality. I am indebted to HarperCollins Senior Commissioning Editor Prema Govindan and her team of editors for having done a superb job with the book and also for accommodating all my requests for pushing the deadlines farthest.

Rajesh Ramachandran

About the Editor

Rajesh Ramachandran is the Editor of *The Tribune*, one of the oldest newspapers of the country, and a former Editor-in-Chief of *Outlook*. For nearly three decades, he has worked with some of India's largest publications and a TV channel, reporting on war and insurgency, and writing on politics, political economy, government affairs and conflict. The edited volume of essays and archival material, *Martyrdom to Freedom: 100 years of Jallianwala Bagh*, published in 2019, was his first book.

-FIRE

km.

WITHIN FIRING RANGE OF INDIAN

Evacuation

Denie

ENDER

TANGAIL, LAKHIMPUR & SITAKUND LIBERATED

Advance Toward Chittagong Being Maintained

NEW DELHI, Dec. 13 (PTI, UNI).— The Indian Army columns racing towards Dacca from three directions were this evening within artillery range of the West Pakistan occupation forces of a division plus trapped in the Bangla Desh capital, an official spokesman said tonight.

AK TANKS, OIL DUMPS IN CHHAMB

Pak Sabre Bombed Orphanage

23 POSTS UNDER OUR CONTROL IN KARGIL SECTOR

UDHAMPUR, Dec. 13 (PTI & UNI).— The

UK To Keep Up Arms Supplies Despite War

CHIEF MINISTER G. M. SADIQ PASSES AWAY

From Our Staff Representative

CHANDIGARH, Dec. 12.— The Jammu and Kashmir Chief Minister, Mr. Ghulam Mohammad Sadiq, passed away at the P.G.I. here today.

The wrapped body of Kashmir Chief Minister G. M. Sadiq is being taken out of the PGI, Chandigarh, on Sunday by Director P. N. Chhuttani and others.

Heavy Fighting Raging Near Dacca And Khulna

CALCUTTA, December 12 (UNI).— Fighting was the key district town of Khulna, as column Desh forces continued to close in on the capital of Chittagong.

ECOGNISES

HISTOR

GREETE

M.P.s Congrat

Fulfillin

OTHER NATIONS

SUIT

INDIAN TROOPS LIBERAT

ENEMY DEFENCE LINES SMASHED

BULK OF PAK FORCES GIVE UP FIGHT, FLEEING

CALCUTTA, Dec. 8 (PTI) — Combined forces of the Indian Army and Mukti Bahini scored yet another signal victory in smashing the Pakistani defence lines and liberating Comilla town today.

The joint columns in the early hours today liberated the Comilla airfield and took hold of the Lalmai heights in a swift move, cutting off all avenues of escape to Mynamati Cantonment, an Eastern Command spokesman told newsmen here tonight.

CEASE-FIRE LINE

KASHMIR

PAKISTAN

PAK HELD KASHMIR

NAYA CHHOR AIRFIELD

IAF gains total air supremacy in Bangla Desh

E FIGHTI

VE ENEMY

S REP

INDIAN ARMY

Gai

l Se

ENEMY

(PTI)—A

NEW DELHI, Dec. 7 (UNI)

Over 2,000 sq. k Captured In

'E. PAK' CABINET

MALIK'S HOUSE DESTROYED

Indian Troops Blast Their Way Into Dacca's Outskirts

DACCA, December 14 (Reuter).— The Government of 'East Pakistan' resigned en masse this afternoon, dissociating itself from further actions of central administration of President Yahya Khan in Islamabad as Indian troops blasted their way into the outskirts of Dacca.

Mr. A. M. Malik, the 'Governor', wrote a shaking ball point pen on a letter to President Yahya with a shaking ball point pen on a of office paper as Indian MIG 21s destroyed his official residence.

Troops Close On Dac